"From the first page, this book feels like an invitation home. By vulnerably sharing her own story of addiction and recovery, Ashley removes stigma and creates a safe, grace-filled space where readers can see themselves and begin to believe that freedom is possible."

Kimberly Haar, LPC, LMFT / Owner of There's Hope! Counseling / Author of *Healing from Life's Deepest Hurts: Reclaiming your Life after Grief, Loss, or Trauma*

"In *Lost No More*, Ashley Martin offers readers a simple but life-changing truth: your troubled past never disqualifies you from God's grace or His will for your life. This book is a brave and unflinching testimony to the redemptive power of God's grace in one woman's life. Ashley, with candor and vulnerability, invites readers into the most painful corners of her story and then lowly and gently guides them toward hope, love, and peace. Jesus never avoids our broken places but meets us there. Readers who have wrestled with addiction, perfectionism, insecurity, or the haunting sense of a "God-shaped hole" will find themselves in these pages. But this is not merely a memoir of recovery; it is a guide to a deeper walk with Christ. The practical emphasis on surrender, prayer, honesty, and spiritual vigilance makes this a resource for anyone longing to move from spiritual numbness to awakened faith. Tender, challenging, and deeply hopeful, this work will encourage countless readers to stop running, step into the light, and allow God to author a new story from the ruins of the old."

Dr. S. Jonathan Bass, Professor of History at Samford University, is a Pulitzer Prize–nominated author known for his numerous books on Christianity in the American South.

"With disarming humor and courageous honesty, Ashley invites us into her story of recovery and transformation. Anchored in God's Word and centered on Christ, this book is a beautiful reminder that real freedom is found in surrender to Jesus."

Carre Coy Phillips, MBA, MBTS / Bible Teacher | Host of *Kingdom Come with Carre Phillips* Podcast

Lost No More

A Daily Path to God in the Midst of Your Deepest Valleys

ASHLEY MARTIN

Library of Congress Cataloging-in-Publication Data

LCCN: 2026906824 (paperback) ISBN: 978-1-961732-38-4 (ebook) | ISBN: 978-1-961732-39-1 (paperback) | ISBN: 978-1-961732-40-7 (hardcover)

Published in association with Called Creatives Publishing, www.calledcreativespublishing.com, Gallatin, TN

Cover design: Called Creatives Publishing
Interior design: Dallas Hodge

2026 - First Edition

Table of Contents

Dedication

For West—

My favorite answered prayer.

Your steadfast belief in me made this book possible.

Introduction

It was an ordinary Tuesday in July. I met a friend for lunch at the Blue Moon, a popular spot in town. Just before opening the front door, I took a deep breath and forced a smile, pretending everything was fine. In reality, my life was falling apart, but I kept the mask firmly in place. Inside, I found my friend, and we ordered at the counter. Finding a table, we sat down, settling into a familiar, light conversation.

Midway through our lunch, two strangers in business suits approached our table. The man locked eyes with me and asked, "Are you Ashley?" When I answered yes, he handed me an envelope and said, "You have been served." Without another word, they turned and walked away. Divorce papers. It was not a surprise, merely a harsh consequence of years spent in a failing marriage and my desperate search for something to fill the void. Rather than confront the pain, I chased relief in an affair. I had made no effort to hide it, had been caught before, and promised to stop, but I did not. Five months earlier, alcohol had stopped numbing the ache. I needed something more substantial to fill the God-shaped hole in my soul, and my choices only deepened the emptiness.

As I sat at that table, holding the envelope in my hand, shame and sorrow washed over me. I had hit rock bottom. In that brokenness, God met me. That night, I cried out, "What's wrong with me?" Hours later, He whispered one word: "Alcohol." That moment marked the beginning of a new life. I have not had a drink since. That was twelve years ago. God used the lowest point of my life to start healing what I thought was beyond repair. What once felt like the end became the moment God began to author a new story—one of grace, redemption, and restoration.

For many years, life felt lost and unanchored. Though I had once known the peace Jesus offers, I drifted away and allowed alcohol to take His place. Everything changed eleven years ago when God whispered to my heart and sparked a spiritual awakening. Since that moment, calling out to my Heavenly Father for daily direction has become essential. The peace and confidence found in Him are not reserved for a select few, they are available to anyone who seeks Him. This book offers a daily path toward our Savior, inviting readers to experience the same steady hope and restoration found in walking closely with Christ.

On this journey you will:

- Not only give God your will, but you will also give Him every situation that lies before you.

- Deepen your prayer life with simple tools and strategies.

- Draw closer to Jesus and lessen your anxiety and fear.

- Learn to manage situations better with prayer and petition.

- Learn to surrender to God's will and gain peace from it.

Whether you have been lost for a season or most of your life, there is always hope of being found. God never left you. You distanced yourself. The Lord is always there to help you find the way back. If there is wreckage from your past, He is there to help clean it up. God is not intimidated by any part of your story. In the end, your Savior will find a way to use your mistakes for His glory. Remember, he left the ninety-nine for one lost sheep.

God is not intimidated by any part of your story.

A Lost Sheep

In the spring of 1993, I was the lost sheep. I had wandered far from the safety and comfort I once knew. That season of drifting began when I was just fourteen, overwhelmed by a cascade of life-altering events I did not know how to process. It started with the death of my grandfather, my favorite person on the planet. His passing shattered me, not only because I loved him deeply, but because I never got the chance to say goodbye. His second wife kept my parents and me from his deathbed, a wound that left a deep scar on my teenage heart.

My grandfather and I shared an extraordinary bond. As his only grandchild, I knew I held a special place in his heart, and he certainly held one in mine. He was my safest place in the world. Every summer, I would spend a week at his house, where he spoiled me with fancy breakfasts, afternoons at the pool, and candy stops on the way home. Back at the house, we would cool off with cartoons until the Alabama heat broke, then head outside so he could push me on the tire swing he built just for me. Those carefree days remain my most cherished childhood memories, and I thank God for them still. But after his death, everything changed.

Not long after, my family faced financial hardship. A bad investment collided with a faltering economy, forcing us to downsize our lifestyle. We moved from a house with a pool into a modest apartment. The nice cars disappeared, replaced by older models. As a young teenager, I could not understand or process these changes. My immature mind internalized the loss, grief, and instability. At the time, therapy for children was not widely accessible or encouraged, especially in the early '90s. So, I did the only thing I knew to do. I went to church. I sought answers, refuge, and meaning in the pews.

I remember looking up at Jesus. He was sketched in the stained-glass window. Robed in white, arms outstretched, floating to heaven-Jesus seemed so far away. I did not reach for Him.

This was eighth grade. My emotions were huge, and I did not know what to do with them. Anger welled up in me. Why was this happening to me? I no longer felt comfortable on that pew. I no longer felt comfortable in my own skin. I felt alone. Drowning in my emotions, I did not cry out to God. I buried my feelings. Sunday mornings, Sunday nights and Wednesday nights, I was present and absent in the same breath. My resentment grew. Then, I entered high school.

At school, my friends talked about weekend parties. I wanted to join them. So, I did. In ninth grade, you must plan your escape. First, I had to find an accomplice. Second, you need a driver. Third step, alcohol.

Mandy was the perfect partner for our plan. She had just moved to town and was eager to meet new people. A bold and lively firecracker from Louisiana, she was always up for a bit of adventure. The plan was simple: we would tell our parents we were watching a movie at Brent's house, even though Brent was actually hosting a field party just down the road. We claimed we had a ride there and back and promised to be safe. After curfew, we would return to Mandy's house and pretend that nothing had happened.

To pull it off, we enlisted the help of someone's older sister to drive us and her boyfriend to buy the alcohol. It was not exactly foolproof; our story had more holes than we realized. By 9 p.m., Mandy's mom had already started to piece things together. By 10 p.m., both of our moms were pulling up to the dirt road party, headlights blazing, ready to haul us home. The night did not go as planned, but it was one we would never forget.

I got my first buzz that night. My belly got warm, and my thoughts got a little fuzzy. The burdens and anger I carried slipped away for a little while. I fell in love with alcohol that night. It became my obsession for the next nineteen years.

I got in trouble, but the reward outweighed the consequences. The next four years were full of bad decisions and regrets. I left high school with a low GPA and no solid plan. But God never gave up on me. I heard His whispers and saw His grace as He saved me repeatedly.

I was lost. Have you ever been lost? It could be for years or moments at a time. Lost in an addiction or losing yourself raising children. Are you lost in your day-to-day routine? Today, are you searching for meaning and a better connection with God?

In the following pages, we will discuss being lost and being found. A plan of surrender and spiritual awakening will be laid before you. All you must do is open up your heart.

You may feel guilty for admitting you are lost in this season of your life. God has blessed you with so much but in the hecticness you cannot hear His voice. You are not alone.

You may have a booming career but at events you feel alone in a room full of people. You no longer feel connected to your Creator. He has blessed you, but loneliness has seeped into your soul. It is time to reawaken your spirit!

You are worthy. You are chosen. You are sought after. Soon you will know your worth.

Let me show you how to seek God daily and spend a little time with Him. Every day will not be a mountaintop experience, but loneliness will fade. Growth will take place. Your spiritual maturity will deepen, and so will your daily dependence on God. New goals will form. This journey will help you create those goals and accomplish them.

You were created with intention. God has woven into your life a unique combination of gifts, experiences, and purpose. Walk the path He has laid before you with humility and trust. No matter what your season of

> **You were created with intention.**

life, continue growing—spiritually, emotionally, and relationally. Keep turning to God, allowing His presence to shape your steps. His plans often unfold slowly, but they are always rooted in His goodness and far exceed our limited expectations.

Do not let the repetition of daily life dull your awareness of His nearness. Invite Him into the ordinary moments and seek Him with consistency. When fear or doubt begins to surface, draw near to Him, He has not moved. In the stillness, He is always ready to guide you forward with grace.

This book will guide you to a deeper, more meaningful relationship with God. God will conquer your daily challenges, not you. At the end of this spiritual awakening, you will feel loved. You will feel found.

Lost

When Running from God
Feels Easier Than Surrendering

*"In God's economy, nothing is wasted. Through
failure, we learn a lesson in humility which is
probably needed, painful though it is."*

—Bill Wilson

July 2013

It was a sweltering July day in Alabama. The temperature
hovered around 100 degrees, with no breeze—just oppressive,
sticky humidity. I sat in the car with my soon-to-be ex-
husband, the air conditioning blasting as we drove to rehab. As
I gazed out the window, my life played out before my eyes. I had
so much promise, yet something always seemed to get in my way.
My PhD remained unfinished, I had sabotaged every meaningful
relationship, and I consistently took advantage of my parents. I
had even abandoned my call to the ministry, allowing alcohol to
take priority. Yes, alcohol was at the core of all my problems. But
now, for the first time in a long time, I had hope. Maybe this place
could help me.

After I admitted I was an alcoholic and needed help, my
husband began speaking to me again. I made an appointment with
my doctor, and within two days, after meeting with a psychiatrist

and getting through a waiting list, I accepted a spot at an inpatient treatment facility.

By the time we arrived in the parking lot, I was no longer nervous, I felt numb. The emotional roller coaster of the past few days had left me completely drained. I had not had a drink in three days, and experiencing my raw emotions while sober was an unusual occurrence for me. Unsure of how to behave, I walked into the building, hoping for the best. After checking in at the front desk, I was called back for my initial intake.

The counselor asked, "Why are you here? How long have you been drinking? How often? How much do you drink each day? What led you here?" I answered truthfully, and it felt good. The weight of shame and guilt began to lift. I had lied for so long that telling the truth had become a rare occurrence. But at that moment, I felt safe. I was sheltered from the world and the mess I had created. So, I kept being honest. Sitting in the conference room, I could almost feel the chains of my sins loosening. I was freeing myself from decades of lies. It had been a dark place, and I had stayed far too long. As the truth finally poured from my lips, I felt myself slowly stepping into the light.

She took my picture. As I smiled at the camera, I felt good about how I looked. My outfit was cute, and my makeup and hair were done. Having recently lost weight gave my self-esteem a boost. Looking back, it is surreal to realize how focused I was on my appearance. Even at my rock bottom, I was still completely self-absorbed. My life was falling apart, yet I was still available for lipstick. I was beginning to change, but I clung to my facade.

After nineteen years of pretending, the transformation was a slow journey, but I was willing. As I smiled at the picture, deep down, I knew the pain was still there. I had not fully processed the damage I had caused to myself and my family. After leaving the intake room, I grabbed my suitcase and said goodbye to my husband. That is when loneliness settled over me.

I sat alone in the waiting room, the silence pressing in as my thoughts swirled. A young woman, who I assumed to be a nursing assistant, finally called my name. Without much expression, she led me down two long flights of stairs into the detoxification center. The air grew colder with each step. The facility looked like a hospital but somehow felt colder, sterile, and uninviting. White walls, white floors, fluorescent lighting, and a front desk staffed by people in scrubs gave the space a clinical, almost impersonal feel. My guide, barely in her twenties, carried herself with quiet toughness. She took me to a small, windowless room, closed the door behind us, and without hesitation instructed me to remove all my clothing.

It took a moment to register. A strip search. There was no room for dignity here. Wordlessly, I slipped off my cute peasant top, shorts, bra, and underwear and placed them on a nearby chair. I felt nothing. I had already spent the morning riding for four hours in a car beside my soon-to-be ex-husband. I had already sat through two grueling hours of questions that left me emotionally depleted. Now, I stood completely exposed, as this petite but no-nonsense young woman in scrubs patted me down like it was just another task in her shift.

That moment stripped more than just my clothing; it stripped my pride. It was one of the most embarrassing, disorienting moments of my life. And yet, strangely, it may have been the first true moment of surrender. I did not argue, resist, or even cry. I just did what she said. Something inside broke open, and maybe, that's when healing began.

Afterward, she took me to a small hospital room and left me alone. A nurse came in a few minutes later to take my blood pressure. It was alarmingly high, and I was immediately given medication. The nurse then asked me many of the same questions the intake counselor had. When she finished, she took me to my room, which had two single beds and a bathroom. My roommate was asleep, so I quietly laid down my suitcase, found my pajamas, and went to bed.

At 3 a.m., I was awakened for a vitals check. I groggily rolled off the hospital bed, put on my shoes, and followed the nurse to a small room with bright lights. She sat at a desk while I took a seat across from her. She asked, "Why are you here?" Without thinking, I answered, "To become the person God created me to be."

The nurse looked at me, astonished, and said, "That's the best answer I've ever heard." I managed a weary smile and replied, "I have no idea where that came from. It is 3 a.m., and I am sitting in detox."

In that moment, a profound truth pierced through the darkness: I was not alone. Even at my rock bottom, God's unwavering light had found its way to me. The disease that had been devouring me from the inside no longer held the upper hand. I was exhausted from running, too weary to pretend I could meet the impossible standards I thought God demanded of me. Then, like a flood, grace washed over me. It was not about what I could offer or how I had failed; it was about a love that did not care how shattered I was. For the first time, I stopped resisting and allowed God in. The hollow shell I had become was finally ready to be filled with something greater. In that sacred moment, I did not just find God. He found me. In the quiet reflection of that moment, I began to see how my story was not so different from others who had encountered God at their lowest points, like the woman at the well.

The Woman at the Well

Now Jesus learned that the Pharisees had heard that he was gaining and baptizing more disciples than John-although in fact it was not Jesus who baptized, but his disciples. So, he left Judea and went back once more to Galilee. Now he had to go through Samaria. So, he came to a town in Samaria called Sychar, near the plot of ground Jacob had given to his son Joseph. Jacob's well was there, and Jesus, tired as he was from the journey, sat down by the well. It was about noon. When a Samaritan woman came to draw water,... (John 4:1-7).

Looking back at that moment—sitting in detox, answering the nurse's questions—I understood the woman at the well: her pain, her weariness, her desperate thirst for something more. Like her, I was burdened with sin, longing for a new beginning yet paralyzed by uncertainty, unsure of where to even begin. Then Jesus appeared. He found her in her brokenness, just as He found me in mine. His questions were simple at first, disarming in their gentleness. But they were not just questions; they were an invitation. An invitation to confront the truth, to face the weight she carried, and to let it go. In that sacred exchange, I see my own story reflected. Jesus did not just stumble upon her; He sought her out. And just like the woman at the well, I came to realize that He had been seeking me all along.

> Jesus said to her, "Will you give me a drink?"
> The Samaritan woman said to him, "You are a Jew and I am a Samaritan woman. How can you ask me for a drink?" (John 4:7-9).

Then he dives deeper.

> Jesus answered her, "If you knew the gift of God and who it is that asks you for a drink, you would have asked him and he would have given you living water." (John 4:10).

Then Jesus gets personal. Leaving the woman vulnerable and teachable. He told her,

"Go, call your husband and come back."
"I have no husband," she replied.
Jesus said to her, "You are right when you say you have
no husband. The fact is, you have had five husbands,
and the man you now have is not your husband. What
you have just said is quite true." (John 4:16-18).

Jesus did not call her out to shame her; he called her up to freedom. He exposed what was hidden not to humiliate, but to heal. There is nothing passive about that kind of grace. It is bold, it is direct, and it changes everything. When we stop hiding and start confessing, we stop surviving and start truly living. Honesty is not weakness; it is the first strike against the chains that keep us bound.

- **Honesty.** I could relate to the honesty of the woman at the well, owning her brokenness. Honesty makes us vulnerable, but it is in that vulnerability that God truly shines. We become humble, and humility is not the same as humiliation; it is an admirable trait our Savior uses to improve us. The woman at the well was honest with Jesus; she admitted her sinful nature. In response, Jesus offered her mercy, grace, and forgiveness. When we are sincere and humble before God, He honors that, especially when we confess our sins and change our sinful ways. You are only as sick as your secrets. I bet the woman at the well suffered mortification. Once she confessed to Jesus, she found new freedom. He did not rebuke her but offered her a new life. Honesty is your lifeline to Jesus.

- **Change.** I recognize the deep desire for change, the longing to accept the invitation Jesus extended to the woman at the well. When He named her truth aloud, He was not shaming her; He was calling her into transformation. Change often begins in the discomfort of conviction. Sometimes it takes being confronted by others, by consequences, or by the Holy Spirit for us to truly see the gravity of our choices. I know what it feels like to persist in sin, even while knowing it is wrong. It is easier to numb, to justify, or to hide than to face the truth. But

> **Change often begins in the discomfort of conviction.**

Jesus does not expose us to wound us—He exposes us to heal.

- **Fulfillment.** In her deep neediness, I sense a profound yearning—a soul searching for something more. Perhaps the woman at the well had tried to satisfy that ache through relationships with men who promised love but left her feeling even more empty. Each time she gave herself away, the disappointment grew, and her sense of worth diminished. Or maybe her story was marked by grief—five husbands lost to death, each one leaving her more alone, more uncertain, more desperate for security and belonging. Whether through loss or repeated rejection, her heart carried the weight of unmet longing. That kind of emptiness is familiar to me. From the age of fifteen through my late twenties, I searched for self-worth in the approval of men. I craved attention and affirmation, hoping they would fill the deep void inside me. Relationship after relationship, I kept hoping someone could complete me, but none of them could. Each one left me more unsatisfied than the last. I was trying to fill a God-shaped hole with people who were never meant to take His place. For years, I believed a lie: that I had to be perfect for God to love me. So, I held back parts of myself, never fully surrendering. But when I finally reached the end of myself, when desperation drove me to my knees, I offered Him everything. No more hiding. No more striving. In that moment of surrender, God met me with the fulfillment I had chased for years. The ache was quiet. The emptiness filled. And the longing I once tried to satisfy through the world was finally met by the One who created me to be whole in Him.

The woman at the well encountered a turning point. Her encounter with Christ stripped away the lies, the secrets, and the shame. She had lived in isolation, likely coming to the well at noon to avoid the stares and whispers of others. But Jesus met her in that place of hiding and gently brought her into the light. His challenge was clear: sin no more. And she responded, not with excuses, but with repentance. She received His truth and allowed it to reshape her life. That is what real change looks like, not perfection, but a willingness to turn around and walk in a new direction. When we surrender our broken patterns, our empty coping mechanisms, and the lies we have believed, something shifts.

The woman left her water jar behind, the very thing she had come for, and ran to tell others about the man who had changed her life. That is the power of grace. Jesus does not just call us out; He calls us forward. Change is not easy, but when it is Spirit-led, it is freeing. Like her, we can step out of the shadows and into a new life, washed in mercy and empowered to walk in truth.

What about you? Have you ever felt insecurities like the woman at the well? Perhaps one unwise decision, or many, has left you feeling embarrassed and ashamed. Instead of inviting God into your life, you might find yourself trying to fill the void in your soul with relationships, food, or other unhealthy habits. You keep reaching for everything but God, and this neediness persists, consuming you. I have been in that place as well, trying and failing to fill my God-shaped hole. I hope my experience resonates with you and encourages you to seek God first. Only our Creator can fill us with the love we need. When the Holy Spirit moves within us, that emptiness disappears. All we must do is invite Him into our daily lives. It took me thirty years to discover this truth.

Hole in the Soul

Middle School c. 1992

The ache in my soul first revealed itself in middle school. I can still see myself—sixth grade, sitting at home, staring out the window with a heaviness I did not yet know how to name. As an only child, I had always been good at entertaining myself, reading books, watching TV, spending hours outdoors in my own imaginative world. But something shifted as I grew older. What once felt like peaceful solitude began to feel like painful isolation. I was not alone anymore; I was empty. Looking back, I now understand what I was feeling: the "God-hole."

The "God-hole" is the spiritual void every human carries, an ache etched into our souls that only God can fill. It is the part of us that longs for meaning, connection, belonging, peace. Ecclesiastes 3:11 says that God "set eternity in the human heart." That eternity-shaped space cannot be filled with anything temporarily, but that does not stop us from trying. Let me ask you: have you ever felt the "God-hole"? That persistent emptiness that no success, relationship, or distraction seems to satisfy.

For me, the "God-hole" surfaced as a deep pit in my stomach, stirring waves of insecurity and emotional restlessness. Puberty brought with it not just physical changes but a slow unraveling of my identity. I questioned everything, my looks, my worth, my place in the world. Was I pretty enough? Popular enough? Seen at all? That hollowness flared up in the quietest, strangest moments—at slumber parties, during youth group games, or in the middle of an ordinary Wednesday afternoon. I did not have the language for it then, but now I know what I needed most was time in God's presence.

There were moments I called out to Him—real prayers, desperate ones—and sometimes, I felt the Holy Spirit flood in, softening the ache, quieting the chaos. But at other times, I ran in the opposite direction. I let the enemy whisper lies and offered my "God-hole" to lesser things: attention, food, compliments, crushes. Eventually, alcohol. Can you relate? Have you ever turned from God, whether for a moment or a season, hoping to find satisfaction elsewhere, only to end up even more empty than before? In that period did the "God-hole" emerge?

Still, my heart lived in tension, torn between moments of sincere pursuit and patterns of self-sabotage, swinging back and forth between reaching for God and running from Him. During that awkward and uncertain season, I usually did seek God. I attended church more regularly. I opened my heart and begged Him to fill the growing emptiness inside me. And for a time, I felt connected, like I was finally getting close to what I had been missing. But then everything changed.

My grandfather passed away. Not long after, we lost our home. Grief and upheaval hit back-to-back, and my young faith was not ready. I did not have a theology of suffering—I only had questions. Why would God take someone I loved? Why would He let our family fall apart? Why would He stay silent when I was screaming inside?

I pulled away from Him. I felt abandoned. Had He stopped listening? Maybe He never had. As I transitioned from middle school into high school, I searched for something to fill the void. I turned to alcohol and relationships, desperate to escape the aching emptiness that had taken root years earlier. What began as a subtle longing became a consuming hunger. I tried to satisfy it with all the world offered: attention, affection, achievement, and escape. But nothing worked. Because nothing ever does, except God. The God-hole only grew deeper. Years later, sitting in a movie theater, I saw that same inner turmoil playing out on the big screen and it hit a little too close to home.

A recent film, *Inside Out 2*, unexpectedly captured this transition in my life with startling clarity. Rarely have I seen a character reflect my own internal struggle so vividly. The main character, Riley, stands on the cusp of high school, and with puberty comes a flood of new emotions—anxiety, envy, embarrassment—all competing for space in her mind. As Riley rides the emotional roller coaster of adolescence, desperately trying to fit in and define her identity, I found myself cringing. Not because it was inaccurate, but because it felt so familiar.

Like Riley, I faced the overwhelming storm of insecurity and confusion. But unlike her, I did not turn toward a healthy resolution, I turned away from God. I began listening to the lies of the enemy, who whispered that God was distant, disapproving, and only interested in perfection. I believed I was too far gone, too flawed for grace. That belief widened the distance between me and my Creator. Instead of seeking comfort in His truth, I numbed my growing fear and shame with alcohol, drugs, and constant social distraction. My heart longed for peace, but I sought it in all the wrong places.

February 1997

Now a senior in high school, there was a growing sense that God was knocking on the door of my heart. By February, resistance gave way, and I attended a Bible study I had previously avoided. Sitting still proved difficult as a strong awareness of God's presence filled the room. Though most memories from those years blur together, this moment remains vivid. The Holy Spirit brought deep conviction—an overwhelming rush of emotion, like electricity surging through every part of me. It echoed the words of theologian John Wesley, who described his own awakening with the phrase, "My heart was strangely warmed."

Have you ever experienced a moment of conviction from the Lord? Maybe it happened while sitting in church, listening to a sermon, or during a quiet moment at a retreat, when suddenly, the weight of your choices hit you, and you realized sin had quietly taken root. That is exactly what happened to me. Over time, I had grown numb to the compromises I was making. What once stirred guilt now felt normal. But in one unmistakable moment, my soul was jolted awake. It was as if a veil had been lifted, and I could finally see how far I had drifted from God's will.

The conviction was an immediate and intensely sharp awareness that the enemy had been gaining ground in my heart and mind. I felt exposed but not condemned. Instead of shame, there was a deep longing for restoration. I did not want to keep living in spiritual numbness. I wanted to come back to the One who knew me, loved me, and was still reaching out to me. That moment stirred something in me that had been buried for far too long, a desire to be clean, to be close to God again, and to live in the freedom only He can give.

Afterward, I stayed to speak with my youth minister. For the first time in years, I confessed my sins openly, releasing the weight I had carried in silence. The act of naming my struggles felt like a breakthrough, something inside me shifted. As I walked out of church that night, I felt lighter, changed. Transformation began immediately. The drinking stopped, my friendships began to change, and before long, I stepped into a leadership role within my youth group. Though I rarely shared the details of my experience, my actions spoke clearly. People noticed a difference, and it was not just outward behavior, it came from within.

In the weeks that followed, the evidence of God's work in my life became undeniable. I experienced more patience, greater compassion, and a growing confidence that had long been missing. A steady peace settled over me. Even my old friends began to comment on the change. Some said they respected my new direction, and a few of those friendships remain today. Every part of my life reflected the truth: God was moving, and I was finally walking with Him.

June 1997

That summer, I went to camp and felt a call to full-time ministry. As a 46-year-old woman writing this, I still remember that night. It was powerful. I knew the call was real, but my eighteen-year-old self was not ready. Fear and self-doubt clouded my conviction, making the call feel distant, like something meant for someone stronger, wiser, or more qualified.

Looking back, I realize I am not alone in this struggle. One thing I have noticed in my life as a Jesus follower is that many of us let opportunities to serve the Lord slip away because of insecurity. Our doubts creep in, convincing us that we are unworthy or unprepared, and we abandon the very things God has called us to do. Maybe it is leading a women's Bible study or helping with Vacation Bible School in the summer. Then the whispers of doubt grow louder. We question our biblical knowledge, ability to lead, and whether we are truly the right person for the task. And just like that, the opportunity slips away, not because God does not equip, but because insecurity tells us otherwise.

I know this battle well because I have lived it. I let my doubts hold me back, and for years, I wondered what might have been if only I had said yes.

From an early age, I felt a stirring in my spirit to serve as a foreign missionary. Raised Southern Baptist, I grew up hearing stories of Lottie Moon, the fearless woman who spent forty years in China sharing the gospel. She was not just a historical figure to me; she was a hero. Every December, I dropped coins into my little rice bowl piggy bank during the Lottie Moon Christmas Offering, imagining it would help someone across the ocean hear about Jesus. The idea of going myself lit a fire in me. I longed to be the hands and feet of Christ in places I had never seen.

But when the time came to take a step in that direction, I froze. I did not know where to start. Missions felt like a calling I did not know how to answer. I did what felt familiar and safe. I stuck with my original plan. That fall, I enrolled at the University of Alabama.

To say I was raised as a University of Alabama fan would be an understatement, I came home from the hospital on a cold January day dressed in a tiny Alabama sweatsuit. Every home my parents owned featured an "Alabama room," a shrine dedicated to Crimson Tide football. The walls were lined with framed photos of legendary players and coaches, commemorative plaques, and vintage posters celebrating iconic moments in the program's history. Crimson and white memorabilia filled every shelf: autographed footballs, miniature helmets, game tickets preserved behind glass, and Bear Bryant quotes in bold lettering. In the corner of the room stands a life-sized, full-color cardboard cutout of Nick Saban, an unexpected treasure my dad scored from a local grocery store's Coca-Cola display, part of a promotional campaign that somehow made its way from aisle nine to our family shrine of all things Alabama. My dad poured his heart into that room, a space that felt more like a museum than a man cave. His greatest dream was for me to attend the University of Alabama, so I did.

August 1997

Attending the University of Alabama wanted to fulfill both a family legacy and a personal milestone, but beneath the surface, I carried unresolved pain and vulnerability that would soon resurface. By the end of August, rush, fraternity parties, and football games ended my sobriety. I did not know then that I was an alcoholic. Drinking made me high or low. There was no in-between. Once I started, I had trouble quitting. I thought that was normal. It was not. The hole in my soul reappeared. My grades started slipping, and my ambition disappeared. After one semester, I got too busy for God. I became depressed because I felt like a failure. How could I have let the enemy back in? Only a few months before, I was on a mountaintop with Jesus, ready to follow Him anywhere.

Have you ever felt this way? While attending a retreat one weekend, you experience a spiritual breakthrough. A realization dawns: a habit, addiction, or unhealthy behavior is causing separation from God. After praying and repenting, a promise is made to the Lord that this behavior will end. The following week, the cycle breaks. When temptation arises, Jesus is called upon. Quiet time begins every morning, followed by prayer throughout the day. Church attendance increases, and a small group is joined. Life feels good. God is being asked to fill the gaps in life that breed insecurity and fear.

Then, a new phase of life begins, and your routine changes. It could be starting college, navigating a busy career, or even raising a family. Whatever the reason, your consistent quiet time with God lessens. You might convince yourself that the peace you find will stick around, even if you are praying less or attending church infrequently. But slowly, your resolve begins to weaken. Suddenly, a tricky situation arises—a major disappointment, a personal loss, or a broken relationship. Instead of seeking comfort and guidance from your Savior, you might find yourself falling back into old patterns. Ashamed of the setback, you pull away from God, and the familiar emptiness returns. This is often the start of a recurring cycle.

- Repeat sin: That familiar pull takes over, and despite your best intentions, you give in again.

- Feel unable to change: A heavy sense of defeat washes over you, convincing you that true transformation is impossible.

- Cycle of guilt: The weight of your actions presses down, leading to a relentless inner turmoil and self-condemnation.

- Tell lies to cover up: Fear of judgment or exposure leads you to hide the truth, adding another layer of burden.

- Full of shame: A deep, pervasive feeling of unworthiness consumes you, making you want to shrink away from everyone, especially God.

- Feel unworthy and unlovable: You find yourself drowning in self-pity without any plan to change. This emptiness only grows larger, consuming you. You turn to alcohol, romantic relationships, nights out with friends, food, hobbies, travel, school, and work as substitutes.

Yet, the emptiness remains at night when you are alone in bed with your thoughts. This feeling is what some might call the "God hole," a void that only He can fill. Only He can keep it filled.

By the end of my first semester of college, I let alcohol back in and shut God out. In my desperation, I called my mom and asked if I could come home. I returned home humbled and looking for direction. I immediately enrolled in a community college. I learned how to study and found a major.

Thriving in a smaller setting, I began to look for a smaller college to enroll in, so I decided on Samford University. Located in Birmingham, Alabama, this institution was the perfect fit for me. It was small and challenging.

January 1999

For the next three years, I opened the door to God again. Though I did not completely shut out my sin, He was working in my life despite me. Academically, I gained confidence in my intellectual ability, made great friends, and maintained a high GPA. To cover my daily expenses, I worked part time at a daycare, took babysitting jobs between shifts, and tutored. My packed schedule kept my addiction somewhat at bay. I drank "only" from Thursday to Saturday, convincing myself it was under control. Those three nights of partying were a blur of reckless choices, each one carving out a deeper hollow in my soul. The harder I refused to surrender to God, the more acutely I felt unworthy and flawed for His plan, propelling me to run even faster in the opposite direction. The idea of a full-time ministry seemed immense, too demanding, too intimidating for someone like me. I was convinced I was too imperfect to fulfill His calling.

We were made to connect with God. Only communion with Him can truly satisfy our deepest longings. We may attempt to soothe our desires with people, food, or alcohol, but the ache always returns. Calling out to God is the only balm for this emptiness, but staying filled requires vigilance. Just like air, food, sleep, and exercise sustain the body, continual praise and connection with God sustain the soul. When we keep the lines of communication open with our Heavenly Father, extraordinary things begin to unfold. And often, He calls us to act. At first, the steps may seem small, holding the door for someone, offering a kind word, or simply sharing a smile. Then, the call grows—praying with a stranger, leading a Bible study, or stepping out in faith with a business venture. When we ignore these promptings, our spirit grows restless and discontented. And sometimes, God will even chase us down.

When we ignore spiritual promptings, our soul grows restless and uneasy. Sometimes, God even chases us down. Remember Jonah, the original runner? His story is not just about a prophet and a storm; it is about any one of us who has ever tried to outrun God.

The O.G. of Running Away

"The word of the Lord came to Jonah, son of Amittai: "Go to the great city of Nineveh and preach against it, because its wickedness has come up before me." But Jonah ran away from the Lord and headed for Tarshish." (Jonah 1:1-3).

God calls Jonah to be a prophet and to preach repentance in Nineveh. However, Jonah refuses and boards a ship sailing in the opposite direction, desperate to flee from God's command. But God is not so easily avoided. In response, He sends a mighty storm, shaking the sea and striking fear into the hearts of the sailors. As the tempest rages, they cast lots and realize Jonah is the cause of their peril. With no other choice, they throw him overboard, and immediately, the sea grows calm.

Then, in a miraculous turn, a great fish, prepared by God, swallows Jonah whole. For three days and nights, Jonah sits in the darkness of its belly, entombed in isolation and despair. There, stripped of all escape routes, he finally turns to the only One who can save him. He cries out in prayer, acknowledging his disobedience and seeking God's mercy. The Lord, ever compassionate, hears his plea and commands the fish to vomit Jonah onto dry land. Humbled and renewed, Jonah sets out for Nineveh and finally fulfills his divine mission, preaching repentance to the people he once feared.

God ordained Jonah, setting him apart for a divine purpose. The standard the Lord called him to live by was not just high; it was a weighty responsibility, demanding unwavering faith and obedience. Then came the call: he was to go to Nineveh, a vast and wicked city overflowing with paganism, to proclaim a message of repentance to a people who neither knew nor feared the God of Israel. The task was daunting. The fear and self-doubt that must have filled his mind were likely overwhelming. How could one man stand against an entire city entrenched in sin? Would they even listen? Would they mock him, reject him, or worse? The burden of such thoughts became too much to bear. So, Jonah ran. He fled from the presence of the Lord, seeking escape from the impossible mission. But as he would soon learn, one cannot outrun the call of God.

Haven't we all been Jonahs at times? God calls us—sometimes in whispers, in undeniable ways—to step into His plans. Yet, like Jonah, we hesitate. Maybe it is simply prompting to give the homeless woman on the street a few dollars and pray with her. Perhaps He is nudging us to step into a leadership role to guide and mentor the youth in our church. Or maybe it is something even more significant, a life-altering call into full-time ministry, missions, or a path that demands sacrifice and faith. Whatever it is, our first instinct is often to question, then to doubt. We weigh the risks, fear the unknown, and sometimes, like Jonah, we run.

Running does not silence the call. It only deepens the conviction. Ignoring it leaves an imprint of regret, lingering knowledge that we have turned away from something greater than ourselves. Yet, just as He did with Jonah, God pursues us. He is patient. Our Heavenly Father is relentless in His love. And even when we resist, He offers grace, returning us to the path He has set before us. The question is: will we listen for the first time, or will we need a storm, a ship, and a great fish to help us answer our call?

I spent years running from my calling, not because I doubted God's power but because I doubted myself. As a young adult, even the basic rules of Christianity felt overwhelming, let alone the thought of serving in ministry. Do not get drunk, avoid sex before marriage, love your enemy—these commands felt like a high bar, an impossible standard. At times, it was too much. I knew I would fall short, so instead of striving for a virtuous life, I chose the easier path of instant gratification. I convinced myself that if I could not be the perfect Christian, I might as well stop trying. My past haunted me, and instead of seeking freedom, I allowed the shame to stay.

What I failed to understand then was grace. Before I grasped its true meaning, I viewed my devotion to Christ through the lens of perfectionism. I believed it was not worth doing if I could not do something flawlessly. The enemy used this to his advantage, whispering lies that trapped me in self-doubt. If I could go back, I would tell my younger self what I know now: Perfection is not the requirement, faith is. At the time, I let fear dictate my choices. I let the fear of failure hold me back from countless opportunities to serve, grow, and embrace the life God had designed for me.

If you have ever felt broken, messy, or too far gone to follow God's calling, you are not alone. I have felt that way too. Like me, you may have believed that if you cannot do something perfectly, then you should not try at all. But here is what I have learned the hard way: God is not asking for perfection; He is asking for surrender. Being lost does not disqualify you; it simply creates an opportunity for grace to do what only grace can do. No matter how far you have wandered or how long you have been running, you can always turn back. God is not waiting to scold you, He is waiting to welcome you. You do not need to have everything figured out. All you need to do is stop hiding and allow yourself to be found.

> **God is not asking for perfection; He is asking for surrender.**

Detour into Doubt

When Faith Fades
and Fear Directs Your Steps

"Perfectionism reflects our natural desire to experience total alignment with our inner and outer worlds."

—Katherine Morgan Schafler

High School, 1993-1997

Looking back, my struggle with perfectionism began subtly in ninth grade, though I did not recognize its true form then. At that age, perfection had a different, tangible shape. It was not merely about being sinless; it was meticulously crafted around appearances. It meant flawlessly dressing in the latest fashion, diligently maintaining a size 2 dress size, and exclusively dating the "right" guy, the one who elevated my social standing.

From my artfully layered "Rachel" haircut cascading around my shoulders to the chunky, unmistakable tread of my Timberland boots, every single piece of my ensemble screamed 90s. My well-worn Levi's jeans served as the perfect, effortless canvas for a loose flannel shirt layered over a form-fitting bodysuit, solidifying my status as the undeniable epitome of the cool, grunge-lite style of the era. The entire "look" was then sealed with a final, deliberate spray of Gap's Dream perfume, its light, fresh scent completing the illusion. I genuinely believed that if I meticulously crafted this outward appearance, I would finally belong.

Sadly, that same flawed, performance, driven thinking seeped into my nascent faith. I began to view church attendance, tithing, and acts of service not as expressions of devotion, but as transactional ways to earn God's favor, as if His boundless love were something I had to work tirelessly to achieve. It quickly became an exhausting, endless cycle of trying to measure up, constantly striving to be "good enough" in His eyes.

As I grew older, I saw patterns in the churches I attended that reinforced this belief. Families who volunteered the most and made significant donations were met with extra warmth and familiarity by church staff. My family, however, did not. It took me a long time to realize I had it wrong.

What I did not realize at the time was that God never asked me to be perfect. It was through my imperfections that He could work miracles. Abraham, Moses, and David were far from perfect, yet God used them in extraordinary ways. So why did I believe I had to chase perfection? My immature mind had allowed doubt to creep in. The enemy whispered lies, and I believed them: *You will never be perfect, so why bother? Just live for the moment and have fun. Christianity is full of impossible rules, do not even try.*

By the time I turned eighteen, I was exhausted from running. I had spent years trying to live on my terms, pushing aside God's calling. Yet no matter how far I strayed, I could not shake the feeling that something was missing. Finally, I surrendered. I told the Lord I was tired of running, and immediately He began working in my life. He opened doors I never could have imagined and mended relationships I thought were beyond repair. God placed the right people in my path, people who loved and supported me in ways I had never experienced. For the first time, I felt I had a purpose.

However, surrendering did not mean my struggles disappeared. My distorted perception of God's love remained tangled with my obsession with perfection. Deep down, I still believed I had to earn grace. So, when I stumbled, falling back into old habits, the guilt became suffocating. I felt as though I had completely let God down, as if my failures could somehow undo His love for me.

Looking back, I wished I had turned to Scripture, cried out to Him, or confided in someone who could have spoken the truth into my life. Instead, I locked my doubts, fears, and insecurities deep inside. Yet the answer had been there all along:

> "But because of his great love for us, God, who is rich in mercy, made us alive with Christ even when we were dead in transgressions—it is by grace you have been saved." (Ephesians 2:4-5).

We cannot earn God's grace; it was freely given to us through Christ's sacrifice, and nothing we do can change that. When we feel distant from Him, it is not because He has left us. It is because we have turned away. Our Heavenly Father never stops loving, pursuing, and offering mercy. It is we who let sin cloud our vision and allow shame to push us further away. But His arms remain open. His grace never leaves; we do.

Even in our wandering, He patiently waits. He does not love us less in our failure or withdraw His promises when we struggle. His grace does not depend on our performance; it flows from His unchanging love. He longs to restore what we have lost, heal what we have broken, and remind us that we can cast our burdens on Him. The enemy wants us to believe that our mistakes define us and that we are too far gone, too broken, or too unworthy to return. But the truth is, no distance is too great for God's redemption. His grace is greater than our deepest sin, and His love is more substantial than our worst shame.

The moment we turn back, even with trembling hands and hesitant hearts, He is already running to meet us. Like the father of the prodigal son, He welcomes us not with condemnation but with celebration. He longs to restore what was lost, heal the broken, and carry our burdens. Grace is not just a second chance; it is an open door, an unshakable promise, a love that will never let go.

For me, that distance came in the form of alcohol. The enemy knew precisely how to reach me. My greatest adversary was not just temptation; it was addiction. I was not ready to let go of it, and I falsely believed I had to choose between God and drinking, as if one misstep would nullify His love. But addiction does not work that way. It hijacks the mind, sinking its claws into every corner of your being. Alcohol became my master, consuming me in ways I never anticipated.

Believing that only the flawless could genuinely follow Christ, perfectionism rose up again to stall me. But the truth is, Christ did not come for the perfect; He came for the broken, the lost, and the ones who could not do it alone. I was precisely the kind of person Jesus died for. And though I had walked away, He never stopped calling me back.

For years, I struggled desperately trying to earn a love that had always been mine. I measured my worth by my ability to follow the rules and convinced myself that I had to deserve God's love. However, grace does not work that way. It was never about my perfection; it was always about Him. God never required flawlessness from me; He only asked for my heart.

Handing over my heart was easier said than done. Self-doubt, a relentless foe, whispered that I would never measure up. Compounding this was my insatiable need to please others. I allowed their opinions to dictate my decisions, and I shaped my identity around their approval rather than God's truth. Yet, the more I chased validation, the emptier I felt.

People-pleasing is a bottomless pit, no matter how much you pour into it; it is never satisfied. The hole in my soul grew larger, and no amount of external affirmation could fill it. Breaking free from this mental trap was not instantaneous. It took years to unlearn the lies I had internalized, to replace perfectionism with grace, and to shift my focus from earning love to simply receiving it. But the journey was worth it. Slowly, God peeled back the layers of insecurity, revealing a truth I had overlooked for far too long: My worth was never in what I did; it was in who He was. This transformation is possible for you too.

1997-2007

From the ages of eighteen to twenty-eight, my relationship with God was inconsistent. In college, I turned to Him only when I needed something; there was no real commitment. I experienced spiritual highs that quickly faded whenever alcohol, drugs, or toxic relationships reentered my life. When I fell in love for the first time in college, I sought happiness in my boyfriend instead of in God.

Unfortunately, the relationship quickly became dysfunctional, and we were both to blame. I left it with my heart broken for the first time, and it would take decades before I could fully commit to another man. During that time, I never thought of turning to God for support. I felt too sinful and questioned why I should even try, knowing how things would end.

The enemy thrives when we surrender to defeat. When we adopt a defeatist mentality toward the Lord, the enemy seizes the opportunity to keep us down, trapping us in a cycle of sin and self-pity. We remain stagnant, never reaching the potential God has in store for us. I know this because I lived it. I refused to change, convincing myself that transformation was impossible. Instead of fighting for the life God intended for me, I stayed in a hopeless state for far too long. Trapped in a cycle of poor decisions and addiction, I felt my life was empty yet did nothing to change it. I believed the path to perfection was too difficult, so I gave up before I even started. Doubt and self-condemnation directed my steps, not God.

Being an Israelite

How many times do we give up on God and ourselves and settle? The story of the Israelites is a powerful reminder of how easily doubt can creep in, even in the face of undeniable miracles. They witnessed God's power firsthand, ten devastating plagues that forced Pharaoh's hand (Exodus 7-11) and the parting of the Red Sea that paved their way to freedom (Exodus 14:21). Yet, by Exodus 16, they were already grumbling about hunger in the wilderness. In His mercy, God provided manna from heaven each morning, but their distrust remained. When Moses ascended Mount Sinai, their impatience overcame their faith, and they turned away, fashioning a golden calf to worship in His place.

> "When Moses approached the camp and saw the calf and the dancing, his anger burned and he threw the tablets out of his hands, breaking them into pieces at the foot of the mountain. And he took the calf the people had made and burned it in the fire; then he ground it to powder, scattered it on the water, and made the Israelites drink it." (Exodus 32:19-20).

Despite all the miracles God performed on their behalf, the Israelites' faith remained fragile. Their inability to trust God's provision reflects a more profound spiritual struggle that reveals a pattern of shortsightedness and fear. They continuously focused on immediate needs and struggles rather than God's long-term promises and faithfulness.

Even after being saved from Egypt's tyranny, they could not see beyond their immediate discomfort. In their impatience, they failed to recognize that God's plans for them were about survival and shaping them into people who would be a testament to His glory and sovereignty. This discontent delayed their entry into the

Promised Land, reminding them how human doubts and resistance to trust can hinder the fulfillment of divine promises.

We take the first job offered after college. We accept a date with an okay guy, so we are not alone on a Friday night-not having enough faith in God to wait for His timing. We stay in a friendship that drains us, afraid that setting boundaries means being unkind— when deep down, we know God is calling us to peace, not people-pleasing. I settled for years, believing I had strayed too far and was beyond redemption. God's love does not have a breaking point. He never stopped pursuing me, even when I resisted Him. His grace found me in my lowest moments, proving that no failure is final when placed in His hands. And if He could redeem me, He could redeem anyone.

> **God's love does not have a breaking point.**

Yet, even as God extended His grace, I struggled to embrace it fully. Instead of walking in the freedom He offered, I redirected my focus elsewhere, pouring my energy into a new dream that allowed me to maintain control rather than surrender. My calling to become a foreign missionary faded away, and a new aspiration took root: I wanted to become a history professor.

Goals often shift in ways we never anticipate. What once felt like a clear, unwavering path can gradually fade, reshaped by circumstances or choices we never intended to make. Joyful milestones, such as marriage or the birth of a child, bring some changes, while pain, loss, or addiction drive others. For me, addiction slowly eroded my sense of direction, steering my life onto a path I never planned to walk.

January 1999-July 2001

During my time at Samford, my experimentation escalated. I dabbled in drugs and experienced my first alcoholic blackouts. My social life was chaotic—I dated frequently, made reckless choices, and found myself in an unhealthy relationship that ended in heartbreak. It was my first genuine experience with emotional loss, but instead of processing it, I sought distraction elsewhere.

Despite my reckless habits, I convinced myself I was still in control. I was not drinking every day, which reassured me that my behavior was manageable. My academic record remained strong—my GPA and recommendations were high—but my standardized test scores were disappointing. As a result, my plans for a four-year Ph.D. program fell apart, and I settled for a solid two-year master's program in history at the University of Alabama at Birmingham instead.

The disintegrating of a dream rarely happens all at once. More often, it slips away piece by piece so gradually that we do not even notice the shift until we are too far from where we started. What began as small compromises eventually led me to abandon my greatest ambitions. My growing addiction clouded my vision, convincing me to settle for mediocrity instead of pushing forward. For years, I regretted those choices, but recovery and therapy helped me understand that my journey, though painful, was not wasted. Today, I have peace, but back then, I was lost, chasing temporary distractions, unaware of how profoundly my choices shaped my future.

August 2001-July 2003

For two years, I juggled three jobs while attending classes, gradually slipping deeper into alcoholism. Even as I maintained high grades, my ambition began to wane. I procrastinated on papers, submitting work I knew was not my best. A few times each semester, I skipped class to party with friends. In those moments, being social felt more important than my future career. I craved instant gratification and believed there was always more time to get serious about my goals. Instead of searching for Ph.D. programs, I drank. As my time at UAB ended, I made no effort to plan for the next step. My dream of earning a Ph.D. no longer seemed significant. Alcohol had become my ruler, and I willingly obeyed.

I was serving another master. Do you ever find yourself putting other things ahead of God? Double-check yourself.

Ask:

1. Did I talk to God this morning before I got on social media?

2. Did I take time to thank God for something today?

3. Did I do something to further God's kingdom today?

The Danger of Divided Devotion

King Solomon immediately comes to mind when I think of someone who abandoned their calling and allowed the enemy to win. Solomon was a man who, when given the chance to ask for anything, chose wisdom. His request pleased God so much that He granted Solomon unparalleled wisdom and poured out additional blessings—wealth, honor, and peace during his reign. Yet, despite his divine gift and favor, Solomon had a weakness the enemy eagerly exploited: women.

> "As Solomon grew old, his wives turned his heart after other gods, and his heart was not fully devoted to the Lord his God, as the heart of David his father had been. He followed Ashtoreth the goddess of the Sidonians, and Molek the detestable god of the Ammonites. So

Solomon did evil in the eyes of the Lord; he did not follow the Lord completely, as David his father had done." (1 Kings 11:4-6).

Solomon's downfall is a sobering reminder that even the wisest are not immune to temptation. The gradual turning of his heart away from God did not happen overnight—it was a slow fade, a series of small compromises that eventually led him far from his original devotion. His story warns us that unchecked weaknesses can become the very thing that leads us astray if we are not vigilant.

It is easy to look at Solomon's life and wonder how someone so wise could fall so hard. But how often do we do the same? How often do we let distractions, desires, or compromises pull us away from God's calling? The enemy knows our weaknesses and will use them against us, just as he did with Solomon. That is why we must guard our hearts, stay rooted in God's Word, and remain steadfast in our faith. Wisdom alone is insufficient, unwavering obedience and devotion to God are needed.

Caught in a cycle of self-destruction like King Solomon, I searched for love and fulfillment in all the wrong places. My dating life and finances were a mess. I never fully committed to one guy and treated those I dated poorly. Scared by past relationships, I feared another heartbreak. Yet, loneliness and the lure of a free meal kept me dating. The weight of my choices suffocated my spirit, leaving me hollow. When not on a date, I spent my money at bars, struggling to pay my bills. I chased fleeting romances, late nights, and the illusion of control—only to feel emptier than before.

The void in my soul grew deeper. I had once found comfort in God, but I searched elsewhere for happiness and came up empty. No matter where I turned, nothing healed the wounds I refused to face. Eventually, I became uncomfortable enough to seek a church home, volunteering occasionally, but I lacked true commitment. Alcohol held me back from fully surrendering to God.

It is easy to let something, or someone, come between you and God. Gradually, you may shift your dependence from Him to a person or an object. Instead of seeking your Savior with all your heart, you may turn to a bottle or another person for comfort. One night, you find yourself unable to sleep and realize that God has become a secondary thought; He feels a million miles away. There is restlessness in your spirit, and you feel empty. The Lord has not gone anywhere, but you have distanced yourself from Him. You know the solution to this emptiness, but you convince yourself that it comes at too high a cost. As you continue to experience failures, you grow tired of striving for perfection. Eventually, you decide it is easier to remain where you are, stuck in sin and mediocrity.

Divided devotion does not always look like outright rebellion, it often begins with just enough compromise to quiet conviction. When we divide our hearts between God and the world, we invite doubt to slip in through the cracks. We start questioning His goodness, His timing, and even His presence. One foot in faith and one foot in flesh leaves us unstable, unsure, and spiritually exhausted. Like Solomon, we may still carry wisdom or gifts, but without complete surrender, we lose sight of the One who gave them. Doubt thrives in divided hearts, but clarity returns when we choose to seek God wholeheartedly, every single day.

August 2003

I know this feeling all too well. Drifting from God rarely starts with outright rebellion—it begins with small, quiet compromises. Skipping a quiet time here, ignoring a nudge to pray there. Before long, your heart grows dull, your spirit restless, and your confidence—both in God and in yourself—begins to unravel. That is exactly where I landed after graduating with my master's in history. I told myself I was just taking a year off. The Ph.D. could wait. I was tired, broke, and burned out from years of academic pressure. I stayed in Birmingham, picking up shifts, waiting tables just to keep the lights on. After work, I drank my way through the night, bar hopping until the early hours of the morning. Gatorade and BC Powder became my daily survival kit.

While my former classmates accepted fellowships abroad and secured spots in prestigious Ph.D. programs, I served tacos and tried to ignore the ache in my chest. I smiled at customers while silently drowning in self-doubt. I used to believe I was smart, capable, and called. But somewhere along the way, that belief eroded. I questioned everything: my future, my faith, my worth. I drank not to celebrate, but to forget. The more I numbed the pain, the deeper the void grew. Watching others rise only intensified the feeling that I was sinking.

In desperation, I began halfheartedly applying for jobs at museums and nonprofit trying to convince myself that something good would eventually come through. But the doors stayed closed. What I thought would be a brief pause became a full-on spiritual standstill. I was not just stuck professionally; I was stuck soul deep. Doubt did not just visit; it moved in. And the more I let it speak, the harder it became to remember the sound of God's voice.

Doubt crept in quietly but took root fast. I stopped dreaming big because, deep down, I did not believe I was enough. Writing, once a lifeline, became a source of fear. The idea of pursuing a Ph.D. no longer inspired me, intimidated me. The Ministry felt laughable. I convinced myself I was not holy enough, disciplined enough, or stable enough ever to be called. So, I numbed the ache instead. I distracted myself with shallow dating, drinking from Thursday through Saturday, stringing one guy along while entertaining another. I was chasing anything that might fill the silence, but nothing did.

Eventually, somewhere between hangovers and heartbreak, I had a flicker of clarity. It was not a grand spiritual awakening, but I managed to sober up long enough to send out a few job applications around the state. That decision did not fix everything overnight, but it was something. A first step. And sometimes, that is all it takes, one small moment of movement when you have been stuck for far too long.

In January, a museum in Mobile, Alabama, offered me a job. I gladly accepted. This job allowed me to use my degree. It had a fancy job title and a big office, too. And Mobile was fabulous! It was an antebellum city on the water with Mardi Gras. I had arrived!

Have you ever stepped into a new job, full of excitement and high hopes, only to realize by day two of training that it is nothing like you imagined? Sometimes, that is just the reality of adjusting to a new role. But other times—and this was certainly true for me—what gets us in the door is not calling or clarity, but ego. We say yes because we want to feel important, chosen, or validated. We walk in with unrealistic expectations, believing the experience will be flawless, that we will thrive instantly, or that the role will fill something empty inside us. When it does not, we are left frustrated and disillusioned, not because the opportunity failed us, but because we placed pressure on it to deliver what only God can.

The excitement did not last long. My salary was low. Between rent, a new car, work clothes, student loans, and wine, I was drowning financially. Then, my job conditions got bad. My boss was not pleasant. I complained to his superiors, which made matters worse. I decided it was time to find a church.

My new church embraced me. To flee my current situation, I decided to be a missionary again. As I researched positions abroad, I attempted to quit drinking. I took a day trip to New Orleans one month into this dry spell. I was drunk within a matter of hours. While bar hopping, I met a boy. We started dating. My drinking was not bad at first, but five months later, the boy and I got into a fight. He hung up on me and never called back. The silence stung my ego, and in my frustration, I spiraled. For two weeks, I went on a bender, drinking heavily to numb the loneliness. One night, I got so drunk that I hit a parking meter with my car and drove away without a second thought. Who does that? Looking back, it is clear I was out of control, but at the time, it never even crossed my mind that I might have a problem.

Sometimes, we are the last to see the truth about ourselves. Have you ever been the last person to recognize something about yourself? Maybe you were in a season of depression, and when someone finally confronted you, it took you by surprise. But after some reflection, you realized they were right. Or perhaps it took a significant event to open your eyes. For me, it was the latter. I was too deep in denial to hear it from anyone else; something big had to happen to wake me up. Yet even after running over a parking meter and narrowly avoiding a DUI, I refused to admit I had a drinking problem. I shrugged it off and kept making bad decisions, distancing myself from God and any sense of accountability.

The hole in my soul grew more prominent with every passing day. I tried desperately to fill it with fleeting romantic relationships and endless rounds of alcohol. But nothing worked. I went through two more boyfriends during this time, treating both poorly and being unable to give or receive love healthily. Meanwhile, my life was crumbling around me—bills piling up, responsibilities neglected, and my sense of self slipping further away.

I was exhausted by the chaos in my life. What I craved more than anything was financial security and the chance to live a wholesome, grounded life. One night, overwhelmed by the mess I had made, I cried out to God, asking for help. My friend Betty once told me, "God cannot move a stationary bicycle." Her words echoed in my mind, and I realized I needed to act.

I began attending church more regularly and contacted the church staff for guidance. Slowly, I started considering a new direction for my life. Instead of pursuing a Ph.D. in history, I began exploring the possibility of attending divinity school. But God answered my plea unexpectedly before I could start the application process.

God sends us lifelines exactly when we need them. I see this as the Lord bestowing His grace upon us, bringing together the right person, place, and time. My minister suggested that I take on a role as a children's and youth minister in Brewton, Alabama. From the moment I arrived, the church family and the entire town welcomed me with open arms. For the first time in years, I felt like I truly belonged. I flourished in my new position, collaborating with the best boss I could have asked for, whose family treated me like one of their own. This experience was the first time I genuinely understood God's grace.

We can never earn God's grace. It cannot be bought, and we cannot lose it. God's grace is not a reward for the righteous; it is a gift for the broken. The sinner is not overlooked, and the weary soul is not abandoned. His grace reaches into the darkest places, offering redemption where there is failure, healing where there is pain, and hope where there is despair. It is free to all—without condition, limitation, or end. No mistake is too great, no past too messy, and no heart too far gone for God's relentless and unshakable grace. All we must do is receive it.

> **God's grace is not a reward for the righteous; it is a gift for the broken.**

The Prodigal Son

No matter how lost we may feel or how far we have wandered, God's grace is always ready to welcome us home. I felt like the prodigal son returning to my Father. God opened every door for me, placing incredible people in my life. Never had I experienced such a sense of belonging and so much love from one community. My story closely parallels the parable of the Prodigal Son (Luke 15:11-32), reminding me of God's unwavering grace.

But while he was still a long way off, his father saw him and was filled with compassion for him; he ran to his son, threw his arms around him, and kissed him. (Luke 15:20).

Like the prodigal son, I had walked away, chasing success and fulfillment on my own terms. My choices, fueled by ego, impulsivity, and a longing for independence, led me further from God. I thought I was in control, but instead, I found myself lost and broken, bearing the weight of my recklessness. My struggles with alcohol mirrored the prodigal son's squandering of his inheritance, an attempt to fill an emptiness that only God could satisfy.

July 2006

Yet, just as the prodigal son reached his breaking point and returned to his father, I, too, reached mine. In my exhaustion and desperation, I cried out to God. Much like the father in the parable, God did not hesitate to welcome me back. His love was unconditional, and His grace was not revoked because of my failures. He provided a way forward, restoring my purpose through a new job, a church family, and a community that embraced me with open arms.

The women in my church became Christ's hands and feet, offering me kindness and wisdom. We spent our mornings laughing over coffee and sharing heartfelt conversations, and profound encouragement. My closest friends, Rebecca and Kerry, became my anchors. Over home-cooked dinners and bottles of wine, we supported each other through life's triumphs and trials. For the first time in years, I felt secure. I found my people.

But even amid these blessings, restlessness crept in. Have you ever achieved everything you thought would bring you happiness, only to find yourself longing for more? That was me. I had stability, friendship, and purpose, yet something felt incomplete.

Comparison became the thief of my peace. I watched friends get married, start families, and build the kind of life I had always imagined for myself. Slowly, insecurity crept in, casting a long shadow over the blessings God had already placed in front of me. I began to believe the lie that I was behind, that I needed a husband to feel whole, and that God had somehow overlooked me. That seed of doubt—quiet at first—grew louder with each milestone I did not reach. Just like before, I allowed discontentment to steer me off course, away from God's perfect timing and provision. Instead of trusting Him to fill the empty places in my heart, I turned to the world's substitutes. I let doubt dictate my decisions, and once again, I walked away from the One who never stopped calling me back.

Doubt has a way of distorting everything—our worth, our timing, even God's character. When we let it grow unchecked, it not only steals our peace but also rewrites our story with fear and falsehoods. Maybe you have been there, too, staring at someone else's life and wondering if God forgot yours. That ache, that longing, that quiet sense of being left behind, it can push us to chase fulfillment in places God never sent us. And that is exactly where I headed next: on a relentless hunt for happiness without Him, only to find that the more I searched, the more lost I became.

Out of the Wilderness

When Rock Bottom Becomes Holy Ground

"Wildernesses are not where God takes us to hurt us—but where He speaks to our hearts."

—Ann Voskamp

Have you ever tried to fill your "God hole" (remember that hole in my soul I described in Chapter One?) with something else? For me, that person was often a boyfriend. I relied on them as my main source of happiness, believing they could meet all my needs. At that time, I lacked confidence in myself and my relationship with God. I did not recognize my worth and ended up giving myself away without much thought.

When it came to my relationship with God, I resisted surrendering to Him completely. Have you ever hesitated to give everything to God? Holding on to a few pieces and refusing to let Him take full control? I did not allow God to guide my dating life, which caused me to bounce from one relationship to another. I used the men I dated, hurt them, and then moved on. Occasionally, they would hurt me first, but most of the time, I was the problem.

Have you ever been consumed by a person? Instead of gradually getting to know someone, you jumped in with both feet and declared it was love? Whenever I started a new relationship, I poured all my free time into that person. They consumed my thoughts, and I found myself changing to win their affection. My expectations skyrocketed. I wanted them to read my mind and fulfill my every need. When they inevitably fell short, I would break things off, creating a never-ending cycle of disappointment.

Do you find yourself learning lessons the hard way? I certainly do. It was not until my time in rehab that I realized God was the only one who could truly fulfill my needs and provide me with lasting peace. I also did not learn the importance of telling the truth and asking for help until my first year of sobriety. At twenty-eight years old, my finances were in disarray, and instead of seeking help from someone, I looked for a husband to solve my problems. That was how my first marriage began.

June 2006

I found him at a wedding. He was one of my high school teachers. While he was teaching me, I never had a crush on him. I was too busy with boys my age. At twenty-eight, I was looking for stability, a man with financial security. My finances were getting messy again. He fit the description. He had never married and was notorious for saving money. We exchanged numbers at the wedding and began talking on the phone. A year later I agreed to go on a cruise with him. By the first day at sea, we were officially dating. One week after the voyage, we were looking for rings. Three months later, we were married.

Initially, I convinced myself that this was God's provision, that He had sent me a husband to rescue me from my chaos. However, deep down, I knew I had not prayed about it. I did not seek discernment or wise counsel. I simply saw an opportunity and jumped at it, hoping it would solve all my problems. Looking back, I realize I confused stability with love and seeking rescue with true redemption. I was not marrying out of a deep, godly connection; I was marrying out of fear and desperation. I was still trying to fill that "God-hole" with something or someone other than Him.

July 2007

Still clinging to the illusion that a new life could fix an old wound, I made yet another big move, literally and emotionally. I quit my job and moved to my hometown. I preferred to teach college classes but accepted a job as a high school history teacher. Change was all around me. Alcohol began calling again.

When I moved into his house, he did not share his walk-in closet with me. His family's personalities were strong, sometimes overwhelming. I ignored all the warning signs and just poured another glass of wine.

Have you ever ignored the signs God placed right in front of you and just kept pushing forward anyway? Maybe deep down, you knew the relationship was not right, but the fear of being alone kept you hanging on. Or perhaps the dread of a hard conversation, and the fallout it might bring, left you stuck in something that was draining your soul. Fear has a way of paralyzing us. But God is so much greater than that fleeting emotion. To come out of the wilderness, you must take a step of faith when He nudges you to move. Obedience is the exit route. And here is the beauty of it: even in the messiest situations, God can bring His goodness.

Unfortunately, at that time, I lacked the faith I have today. I allowed fear to guide my choices and let the enemy win by stepping into a marriage that did not have God at its center. The stress only compounded. On top of the challenges within the marriage, I moved to a new place and started a new job. Yet instead of inviting God into my struggles, I ignored Him.

I started drinking more to numb my discomfort instead of confronting it. At work, I forced a smile through gritted teeth, and at home, I played the role of the happy newlywed. But inside, I fell apart. I sensed that something was wrong, yet I could not bear to face the truth. Admitting I had made a mistake felt too heavy and humiliating. So, I poured another glass, hoping it would quiet the noise in my mind just enough to get through another day.

Walking with Nonbelievers

"Do not be yoked together with unbelievers. For what do righteousness and wickedness have in common? Or what fellowship can light have with darkness? What harmony is there between Christ and Belial? Or what does a believer have in common with an unbeliever? What agreement is there between the temple of God and idols? For we are the temple of the living God. As God has said: "I will live with them and walk among them, and I will be their God, and they will be my people." Therefore, "Come out from them and be separate," says the Lord. Touch no unclean thing, and I will receive you." (2 Corinthians 6:14-17).

Ignoring warning signs never works. God calls us to partner with those who will uplift, challenge, and draw us closer to Him. When someone loves Christ, they show love in a unique way. There is an abundance of compassion and mercy. While selfishness will always be a temptation, we must strive for Christ to shine through in our relationships.

Paul's words in 2 Corinthians are not limited to marriage or romantic relationships; they apply to all areas of life where we form deep partnerships. This includes business, close friendships, and the influences we have on our hearts. Aligning ourselves with those who do not share our faith can lead us away from God's path.

We are not called to avoid non-believers, Jesus Himself dined with sinners and pursued the lost, but we are called to discern the difference between ministering to others and becoming entangled in relationships that pull us away from God. When we prioritize spiritual compatibility, we create space for God's presence to flourish in our lives. It builds a foundation rooted in faith rather than compromise. Choosing to walk in the light means intentionally surrounding ourselves with people who reflect His truth, not those who diminish it. This is how we begin to come out of the wilderness, that barren place of fear, shame, and spiritual confusion. We step back into communion with God by choosing relationships that draw us closer to Him, not further away. When we align our hearts with His, even our connections begin to carry the evidence of redemption and restoration.

Reflecting on my past, I deeply regret not heeding the profound wisdom of Scripture. I chose a partner who, while a Christian, kept his faith private and never encouraged me to prioritize God. He was not actively involved in a local church and seldom discussed his faith. I accepted this without question, my only request being that we attend the First Methodist Church in town. However, for us, this became more of a social routine than a true spiritual commitment.

Without realizing it, I allowed my intimate connection with God to slip away. Wine became my constant companion, filling the void that should have been occupied by spiritual accountability. He never offered it, and I never sought it. Before I knew it, God had become a distant memory in our marriage.

Yet, in His boundless mercy, God used even my mistakes to teach me. I now grasp the vital importance of being equally yoked. True peace is not found in comfort or convenience, but in obedience. When we trust God enough to wait for His best, we can avoid unnecessary pain. He knows our true needs far better than we ever will.

In time, it became painfully clear that our marriage could not be healed in the state we were in. We went our separate ways, and I entered a new season—still wounded, still searching for security, and still trying to fill the emptiness in my heart with anything but God. Though the chapter ended, I carried the same unresolved hurt, the same fear, and the same patterns into the years that followed.

July 2013

I entered a new season of life yoked to someone who acknowledged God but was uncomfortable sharing his faith with me. We went to church together, but it felt more like a performance than a partnership. I joined the choir while he sat in the back row reading the newspaper. I said nothing. Fear became my constant companion. I was so eager to belong that I compromised my convictions. Somewhere along the way, I stopped asking if God approved. I only asked if things looked good from the outside. Like the Israelites (see Numbers 14:1-4) wandering in circles, I let fear of the unknown and desire for control keep me stuck in a spiritual wilderness.

That summer, everything changed quickly. I started a new teaching job that offered a generous salary, retirement benefits, insurance, and summers off. It looked like a dream on paper, but it quickly became overwhelming. I had never taught high school before, and it showed. By week three, I managed to get a handle on classroom discipline, but I never felt like I could let my guard down. Every day left me emotionally drained. I missed my old town, my church, my spiritual footing. The wilderness was not just a metaphor; it was my daily reality.

The wedding was set for September. I wanted to elope, but he wanted a big wedding. I gave in. Planning the event kept me busy and distracted. The ceremony was lovely. Friends and family came. We postponed the honeymoon until Thanksgiving. I clung to the hope that this marriage would somehow make me whole.

Just one month later, I found out I was pregnant. I was overjoyed. But within days, I began to cramp and bleed. At the ER, the doctor said it was too early to confirm anything. I returned to work the next day, pretending everything was fine. But it was not.

I miscarried at work in the computer lab with my co-worker Vicky and a room full of students. Stunned and broken, I finally agreed to go home and heal for the next few days. Then came a second blow: my husband admitted he no longer wanted children. As an only child, all I had ever dreamed of was having a large family. I did not know what to do. I wanted companionship, financial security, and stability. I was not ready to give that up. So, I decided I would change his mind.

Have you ever found yourself in a situation where you tried to change someone, believing that persistence or love could shape their heart? It is a struggle we all face at some point. For me, it was a battle between faith and control. I lacked the faith in God and the confidence to believe that He could create a better life for me. Like Sarah, who took matters into her own hands instead of trusting God's promise (Genesis 16), I tried to force a future I was never meant to manipulate. Have you ever let fear instead of faith shape your choices?

Over the next six years, I tried everything—emotional appeals, logic, even silence. I waited and hoped my ex-husband would change his mind about having children. In the meantime, I buried my emotions and drank daily. Alcohol dulled the ache, but it could not erase the emotional and spiritual pain I was feeling. At work, I counted the hours until I could get home to my martini. I told myself I was not an alcoholic because I could wait until 3:30 p.m. That lie kept me bound.

Years later, my ex-husband admitted that after my miscarriage, he was terrified another pregnancy would end in more loss. He did not want us to endure that heartbreak again—the physical, emotional, and spiritual toll felt too heavy. At the time, he did not share these fears. Instead, he shut down, believing silence would protect us. But the silence did not shield our marriage; it slowly suffocated it.

Of course, there were good moments too—cruises, holidays, laughter with friends. I enjoyed his family, and my parents adored him. These moments brought joy and hope, but underneath it all, I was still crumbling. I longed to have children. He did not. So, I drank.

One night, I attended a party and promised myself I would only have two glasses of wine. But as I poured my third, something inside me whispered: You cannot stop. I ignored it. I buried it. I kept drinking.

Ignoring a problem does not make it go away. It makes it grow. Whether it is addiction, control, people-pleasing, or an unhealthy relationship, pretending it is not there only prolongs the pain. Proverbs 14:12 says, "There is a way that appears to be right, but in the end, it leads to death." I refused to admit the truth, even as my choices hurt others, damaged my health, and stole my peace. But thankfully, God was not finished with me. My wilderness was about to reach its end.

Fall 2012

The last year of our marriage unraveled quickly. We were both responsible in diverse ways, but I can now admit that much of the damage stemmed from me. My husband buried himself in work and hobbies, shutting down emotionally. I spiraled deeper into self-destruction.

Alcohol no longer numbed me enough. I wanted something more. Convinced I had ADHD and was desperate to lose weight, I sought out medication. The warning label was clear: *Do not mix with alcohol.* I ignored it. I was unraveling fast. My moods shifted. My temper exploded. My resentment boiled over, feeding the anger I had refused to confront. My wilderness had turned into a desert of despair.

January 2013

Then came my birthday. My ex-husband's love language was not gift-giving, and I told him it did not matter to me. The truth was it did. Instead of sharing my real desire, I kept it buried and allowed it to fester. That January, I walked into a jewelry store and picked out a beautiful garnet ring. It was not just a gift; it was a quiet act of self-worth, a small token to remind myself that I mattered. That evening while cooking dinner, I showed it to my husband. We had an agreement that we would not make a purchase of over $500 without discussing it with one another. Since I had not spoken to him at first, he asked me to return it.

At that moment, something inside me broke. My ex-husband had not just dismissed the ring; he had denied me. In that instant, I knew our marriage was over. My heart was no longer in the marriage. An hour later, I left to teach a night class, my emotions too raw to trust my own voice. Instead of lecturing, I handed my students a writing assignment, dismissed them early, and sat alone in the empty classroom, staring at the walls in numb silence.

The end of a relationship rarely occurs in a single, dramatic moment. More often, it unravels quietly, one disappointment at a time, until love withers in the shadows of neglect and indifference. My marriage did not end with an argument or a legal document; it ended in my heart, in that dark and lonely place where hope faded into resignation. I lost all compassion for my husband. We were no longer a team, partners. And instead of seeking reconciliation, instead of asking for a divorce, instead of turning to God, I drank.

> **Placing your self-worth in another person is a losing battle.**

Placing your self-worth in another person is a losing battle.

People will let you down. I had spent years trying to change my husband, expecting him to fill a void only God could fill. But no human being can bear the weight of another's unmet expectations. True contentment and peace come from Him alone. Happiness is fleeting, but faith in our Savior brings the lasting serenity that makes life worthwhile. Yet rather than surrender my pain to God, I buried myself in work and drowned my sorrow in alcohol, desperately trying to silence the ache that only He could heal.

At the time, I was juggling a full-time high school teaching job, coaching cheerleading, and teaching two college night courses. I had no idea how much I earned. None of it mattered. The only numbers I cared about were the ounces of wine in my glass or the vodka in my bottle. Paralyzed by fear, I did not leave; I just stayed miserable. I buried my emotions, spoke to no one, and let alcohol become my closest companion.

Self-pity is a common and easy trap to fall into, and it can be challenging to escape. Instead of taking steps to change, you might find yourself sinking deeper, convincing yourself that no one understands you and that life is unfair. Misery becomes familiar, and negativity feels like the only certainty. That was my experience. I allowed self-pity and alcohol to define my life, but eventually, even they were not enough. I craved something more, an adrenaline rush to escape the emptiness.

February 2013

A month later, I found my next escape. I attended a party alone, where I met a man. We spent time together that night, and he asked for my number. Within two weeks, we were deep into an affair. He flattered me, bought me gifts, and made me feel seen. Desperate for validation, I convinced myself this was what I needed. I stopped going to marriage counseling, telling myself I had already found the answer. But deep down, I knew I was clinging to yet another false fix. Like the Israelites wandering in the wilderness, I was chasing comfort while drifting further from the Promised Land.

Three months into the affair, I stood in front of the mirror getting ready for school and did not recognize the woman staring back at me. Her eyes were hollow. Her spirit dim. She looked like a stranger wearing my skin. For a moment, I could not breathe. But instead of confronting the truth, I buried my feelings and numbed them with routine. I wanted to believe I was still in control, that I could manage the affair, the drinking, and the double life. But every smile was a mask, and every laugh was a lifeline stretched too thin. I had strayed so far from the woman God created me to be. And yet—even in the shadows, His voice was still there. Gentle. Steady. Whispering me home. But I was not ready to follow it yet. Doubt had become my wilderness, and I still thought I could find my own way out.

July 23, 2013

By then, part of me wanted to be caught. Living in deception is exhausting, and I believed my husband had known the truth all along. After five painful months, he handed me divorce papers. That night, I moved in with my parents. It was my rock bottom, the moment everything unraveled. That evening, I had my last drink of alcohol. I crawled into bed with a question: "God, what is wrong with me?" And sometimes in the stillness of the night, He woke me. I did not hear a booming voice. I heard one word: *alcohol.*

Have you ever had God whisper something to your spirit so clearly it stopped you in your tracks? Not a loud voice, not a lightning bolt, but a quiet truth that pierced through the noise. For me, that moment came on July 24, 2013. In a single instant, He named what I had spent years denying: *alcohol.* The fog of denial lifted, and I could no longer pretend. Psalm 32:5 says, "Then I acknowledged my sin to you and did not cover up my iniquity. I said, 'I will confess my transgressions to the Lord.' And you forgave the guilt of my sin." That verse became real in my life. The next morning, I was ready to ask for help. It was not easy. But it was necessary.

Let me ask you: What has God been whispering to you? Is there something you have been avoiding, denying, or burying deep? Where are you still wandering in your own wilderness, searching for peace in places that only leave you emptied? What would happen if you finally named it, laid it down, and asked Him to meet you in that vulnerable place?

That moment of honesty cracked something open inside me. For the first time in decades, I told the whole truth—no filter, no façade. I sat in a counselor's office and exposed everything: the drinking, the affair, the shame. It felt like emotional whiplash. One minute I was raw and real; the next I was trying to put my polished teacher mask back on. I was terrified. I had spent twenty years drinking away emotion, and now I was pouring my soul out to a stranger. Have you ever felt that tension, longing to be healed but afraid of what healing might require?

I did not know what would come next, but I knew I could not keep living the way I had been. I was completely drained—physically, emotionally, spiritually. Everything I had used to define myself had fallen apart. I was no longer a wife. No longer the accomplished, well-dressed woman behind the podium. I was simply a broken daughter of God, desperate for restoration. And yet, even in that low and lonely place, I felt something I had not felt in years: hope. Maybe surrender was not weakness. Maybe it was the *path out of the wilderness*, the first step into freedom. Isaiah 43:19 echoed in my soul: "See, I am doing a new thing! Now it springs up; do you not perceive it? I am making a way in the wilderness and streams in the wasteland."

Rehab became my classroom, and God became my teacher. Each day brought a new lesson—not just about addiction, but about grace, truth, and identity. I learned that healing is not a one-time event. It is a daily choice. Shame began to lift as I replaced lies with scripture. Slowly, I started to see the woman in the mirror not as a failure, but as someone God was still delighted in. As my body detoxed, my soul detoxed too. I had to release the old to make room for the new. That was my second crossing out of the wilderness, not just from addiction, but from the lie that I was too far gone to be redeemed. Have you done that soul work? What lies are still living where truth belongs in your life?

I thought I would walk out with a simple outpatient plan. But after hearing the full story, the counselor looked me in the eye and said, "You have been drinking nonstop for nineteen years. You need inpatient treatment." Her words stung, but I knew she was right. That was the moment I fully surrendered. I stopped fighting. I stopped pretending. I finally said the words I had run from for years: *I am an alcoholic.*

With that confession, peace flooded in, peace unlike anything I had ever experienced. My Shepherd had found me in the wilderness. And this time, I followed Him out. So now, let us talk about you. How can my story of doubt, shame, surrender, and recovery help you draw closer to God in your everyday life? What have *you* tried to use to fill the "God-hole"? Where do you feel lost or stuck in your wilderness?

In the chapters ahead, I will help you crystallize what I have learned from my journey. I will show you how to build a practical, daily pathway to God—through surrender, prayer, and service. These are not complicated steps or spiritual checklists. They are the rhythms that saved my life and anchored me back to the Father's love.

Let's walk this road together. The path forward may not be perfect, but it will be holy. And it begins with your next step.

The Lord Is My Shepherd

"The Lord is my shepherd, I lack nothing. He makes me lie down in green pastures, He leads me beside quiet waters, He refreshes my soul. He guides me along the right paths for his name's sake." (Psalms 23: 1-3).

Nothing compares to the moment you realize that God has intervened to rescue you. You look around and feel, without a doubt, that your Heavenly Father loves you so deeply that He paused everything to save you. First comes relief—your heart exhales. Then, awe washes over you, followed by an overwhelming wave of emotion, whether it is tears or a lump in your throat. But deep down, you know. It was Him. It was always Him. You feel loved, cherished, and truly seen by your Savior.

That is precisely how I felt when God took my hand on that hot July day and led me to my green pasture. Some might call me crazy for seeing rehab as a place of peace, but for me, it truly was. In that space, stripped of distractions, I found rest—proper rest that seeps into your soul and renews what is weary and broken.

Where is your green pasture? Where do you need rest? Perhaps your perfectionism at work keeps you up at night, the weight of expectations pressing on your chest. The stresses of motherhood might overwhelm you, leaving you with doubt and insecurity. Or you might be carrying a secret burden too heavy to bear alone. Whatever it is, your Shepherd sees you. He calls you to lie down in His presence, to step away from the chaos, and to let Him lead you beside quiet waters.

His love is your refreshment. The world will drain you, demand more, and convince you that you must earn rest. But God is different. He longs to pour into you, to quench your thirst with His goodness. Bask in His presence and let Him restore your soul.

His path always leads to peace. Allow Him to guide you. Surrender to His goodness.

I speak from experience. As I began my path to recovery, the God-shaped hole in my soul slowly started to fill. Stepping out of the shadows and exposing my secrets was terrifying, but with each truth I faced, the weight on my shoulders lightened. The road was not easy. I had to confront my past, make amends, and accept the consequences of my choices. My marriage ended, and my life looked different from what I had planned, but through it all, my Shepherd never left my side. At night, when I laid my head down, I did so sober. For the first time in years, my soul was truly refreshed.

However, my renewal did not come from a change in circumstances. My spirit regained strength as I allowed the Lord to meet me in my brokenness. I stopped trying to navigate life independently and surrendered my thoughts and actions to Him. For the first time, I let God lead me, and I listened. I listened to His direction, guidance, and voice in the quiet. Even though I was walking through a dark valley, my Shepherd continued to guide me.

> "Even though I walk through the darkest valley, I will fear no evil, for you are with me; your rod and your staff, they comfort me. You prepare a table before me in the presence of my enemies. You anoint my head with oil; my cup overflows. Surely your goodness and love will follow me, all the days of my life, and I will dwell in the house of the Lord forever." (Psalms 23:4-6).

Where do you find yourself in this Psalm? Are you in need of rest, longing for peace? Or are you walking through a dark valley, desperate for comfort? Perhaps you are somewhere in between, craving guidance but feeling hesitant to surrender control. Wherever you are, do not fear; you are not alone. Your Shepherd is near, and His presence is steady and unwavering. The Holy Spirit never leaves you. Remember to call on Him. Spend time with your Savior.

Welcome the Lord in and acknowledge His presence. Let go of your worries, comparisons, and "what-ifs," and simply be with Him. If you are feeling overwhelmed, take a pause and shift your focus. Instead of dwelling on what is lacking, begin to count your blessings. Write them down and reflect on the many ways God has provided for you. Can you see that your cup is still overflowing?

Now, set aside your lists and listen. Close your eyes and open your heart. Shut out every distraction and dwell in God's goodness. Let negative thoughts fade away, replaced by the warmth of your Savior's love. Do you need guidance? Words of encouragement? Or simply the feeling of being loved? Whatever it is, the message will come. Turn off the noise of the world and listen; your Shepherd is calling. Sit in His presence and draw in God's goodness and grace.

The Good News

We all get lost in the chaos of life. In the noise, the doubt, the pain, we begin to believe the lies of the enemy: that the world will satisfy us, that God expects too much, that we will never be enough. But here is the truth: our Father does not shame or reject us; He invites us home. In His presence is peace. Only His presence heals the ache nothing else can fill.

> **Only His presence heals the ache nothing else can fill.**

If you have seen yourself in *Lost*, wandered with me through the *Detour into Doubt*, or felt the ache of being *Out of the Wilderness* but not yet fully home, take heart. You are not alone. God never left you, not for a moment. When we feel far from Him, it is usually because we have stopped looking, not because He has stopped loving. The way *out of the wilderness* is not complicated. It begins with a choice: to return. To confess, to lay it all down, and to start walking a new path. One step at a time.

That is what the next three chapters are all about laying down a daily path to God through surrender, prayer, and service. These are not rules; they are lifelines. They are the three pillars I live by. It is how I began to reconnect with God after years of drifting. I started small: surrendering what I could not change, writing down what I could, and setting goals that aligned with His will, not mine. I learned to pray, not perfectly, but persistently. I invited God into my mornings, into my stress, into my decisions. And I began to serve, not out of obligation, but out of overflow. Helping others got me out of my own head and closer to the heart of my Heavenly Father.

Maybe life feels heavy for you right now—grief, addiction, regret, or just the daily exhaustion of trying to keep it all together. Or maybe you are a long-time believer who has been faithful but stretched thin between your children, your husband, your job, and your aging parents. You are running on fumes. You love God, but you are wondering how to find time for Him, and if you even have anything left to give.

Friend, this is where the shift begins. These next three chapters are not just teachings. They are invitations. Invitations to come out of the wilderness for good. To step into a daily rhythm with God that brings peace, purpose, and renewed faith. When you practice surrender, prayer, and service, something changes. The Holy Spirit begins to rewire your perspective. You wake up asking, "God, how can I serve You today?" And that simple question will change everything.

So how do you make this real? The answers are waiting on the next pages. You will find practical tools at the end of each chapter: space to reflect, prompts to pray, and ideas to put your faith into action. Start small. Craft a morning prayer. Write a list of things you need to surrender. Think of just one way to serve someone this week and do it. When you add these touchpoints throughout your day, the Holy Spirit will meet you there. You will begin to see His presence in places you once overlooked. Gratitude will grow. Joy will return. And your faith will deepen in ways you never expected.

And do not worry; this path is not about perfection. God does not need a perfect performance. He wants your presence. Some days, your prayer may just be a whispered "Help me." And that is enough. On other days, you will overflow with praise. What matters most is showing up. God values consistency more than checklists. He sees your heart, not your to-do list.

When you begin walking with Him daily, you will start noticing His fingerprints everywhere—in the chaos, the quiet, and even the cracks. That is where real transformation begins. The good news? He is already here. He is waiting. Let's begin.

Surrendering the Compass

Freedom Found in Letting Go

*"Our desire for control—for logic, for reason,
for that which makes sense to us—is one of the
biggest factors in why we don't have more God."*

—Lisa Whittle

Before embarking on any journey, I ensure I am well-prepared: I gather directions, supplies, and even a playlist for the road. I do not set out unprepared, especially if I anticipate challenges. The same level of preparation is necessary for the spiritual journey of surrender. Letting go and allowing God to lead is not a spontaneous emotional act; it requires intention, trust, and a daily commitment to faith. This sense of readiness equips us for the journey ahead.

Surrender is not a one-time event but a lifelong practice. Each day we are faced with the choice to let God lead, even when fear and temptation press in. This kind of surrender is rooted in faith, not only in what God can do, but in who He is: faithful, sovereign, and good. It also means releasing the past. Our history does not define us, because God's grace frees us from shame, regret, and the lie that we are too broken to be used by Him.

But surrender does not stop with our struggles; it also includes our blessings. God invites us to place even the good gifts into His hands, relationships we treasure, dreams we have worked hard for, or successes we take pride in, acknowledging that they all belong to Him. Surrender also asks us to resist the urge to control: to release manipulation, self-justification, and comparison. These may look like control, but they are only counterfeits, and surrender silences them. When we finally place both our struggles and our successes in God's care, we do not lose strength; we gain peace. Strength begins the moment we let go.

> **Strength begins the moment we let go.**

Surrender Involves a Daily Choice

"Submit yourselves, then, to God. Resist the devil, and he will flee from you. Come near to God and he will come near to you." (James 4:7-10).

August 2013

It was my second week in rehab. I sat in the chilly cafeteria, wrapped in a sweatshirt, clutching a cup of coffee like a shield against the cold and the chaos inside me. The air conditioner hummed above, too cold for comfort, but somehow, its drone matched the fog inside my head. A guest speaker had come to share her story—her experience, strength, and hope. She admitted drinking Listerine at work to get high. I rolled my eyes. I was bored, restless, counting the minutes. Then, quiet as a breath, felt it. A whisper from God: "Find one lesson in her story to take with you." So, I listened, really listened. And when she finished, something in me had shifted.

We lined up single file to head downstairs to the pharmacy for our nightly medication. The hallway was dim, institutional, humming with fluorescent lights. I remember thinking, *I hate following rules*. And then, that voice again, gentle but piercing: "Not following rules got you here." It hit me like a flood. I could not live the way I had anymore. I could not keep fighting the structure, the boundaries, and help from others. If I wanted to stay sober, I had to do something radical. I had to change everything. So there, in that hallway with its dull red tile floors and walls that smelled faintly of antiseptic, I surrendered. Not halfway. Not with conditions. I handed God my whole heart, my entire broken life. No more bargaining, no more pride. Just surrender. And in that quiet moment, waiting for my blood pressure medication, everything began to change.

That moment in rehab was my first real surrender—raw, unpolished, and utterly necessary. But surrender is not a one-time event. It is a choice we return to daily, a posture of the heart that keeps us open to God's leading. The key to making that choice repeatedly is faith.

Surrender Requires Trusting God

"Now faith is confidence in what we hope for and assurance about what we do not see." (Hebrews 11:1).

In early sobriety, my faith in God and His plan was the anchor that kept me steady. For the first time in my life, I trusted Him fully, not just with the big picture, but with every detail of my days. I surrendered everything and prayed constantly for His guidance, finding solace and strength in each prayer. During that season, men began to ask me out, including my ex-husband. He is a good man, and choosing to return to him would have been both familiar and easy. For a moment, it seemed like reconciliation might be the path forward.

But I prayed earnestly for God to direct my steps, and He answered in a way I could not ignore. On the first evening we had dinner together, I felt a deep unease, a sick feeling in the pit of my stomach. When it happened again a few days later, I recognized it as God's gentle but firm redirection. Trusting Him and His plan, I told my ex-husband we would not be getting back together. In that instant, the nausea lifted. Six months later, I met West, the man who would become my husband, a testament to the beauty of God's plan.

Faith is the foundation of surrender. We trust not only in what God can do but in who He is, faithful, sovereign, and good. This trust does not erase the questions or remove the struggle; it gives us courage to let go anyway. I have seen it on my own journey through recovery. Do I know what is ahead? No. Do I question Him? Absolutely. Yet I know that surrender means placing even my uncertainties in His hands.

Hebrews 11:1 emphasizes that faith is confidence in our Savior. Even though we cannot see Him, we know He exists. We can feel His presence through moments of peace and conviction. When we look back over our lives, we can recognize God's fingerprints everywhere, making it hard to deny His existence. What key moments in your life illustrate God's faithfulness? I think of my path to rehab, finding my husband, and the birth of my son, Grant. God showed up in powerful ways. So why do I still struggle with surrendering? Because I am human! I have a desire to control. I need constant reminders. Thankfully, the Bible is full of evidence of God's faithfulness.

> "By faith Noah, when warned about things not yet seen, in holy fear built an ark to save his family. By his faith he condemned the world and became heir of the righteousness that is in keeping with faith. By faith Abraham, when called to go to a place he would later receive as his inheritance, obeyed, and went, even though he did not know where he was going." (Hebrews 11:7-8).

In Hebrews 11:7–8, the writer illustrates the essence of faith through the lives of two men, Noah and Abraham. Both faced circumstances that defied human logic, yet they chose to trust God completely. Their stories reveal that faith is not passive belief but active obedience, even when the path ahead seems uncertain.

The verses highlight how both Noah and Abraham responded to God with radical obedience, even when the future was uncertain. Noah trusted God enough to act on a warning no one else could see, and Abraham left everything familiar to follow a promise he could not yet grasp. Their faith was not passive belief but active surrender—demonstrating that true faith is a call to action, even when the outcome is unclear.

Noah, for instance, stands as a monumental figure in the realm of faith. When God commanded him to build an ark, Noah was not merely following a simple task; he was responding to a divine mandate that seemed utterly absurd to those around him.

Imagine the scene: Noah, amid a vast, arid desert, with no sign of the cataclysmic flood coming. With unwavering resolve, he began constructing an enormous vessel purely on faith. This act alone was a testament to his character. He gathered two of every kind of animal, dedicating years to the laborious task of building the ark, all while facing incessant doubt and ridicule from his neighbors. "Why build an ark?" they must have scoffed. "What is rain?" Yet, Noah remained steadfast, driven by a commitment to fulfill God's will. His extraordinary faith was underscored by the total surrender of his life, future, and family to God's plan. Because of his obedience, the Lord not only ensured Noah's safety during the flood but also gifted him the sign of the rainbow, a powerful symbol of God's unyielding faithfulness and the promise that the earth would never again be destroyed by flood.

Turning to Abraham, the writer of Hebrews highlights another profound example of faith. Often referred to as the father of faith, Abraham's journey was marked by unwavering trust in God's promises. When God called him to leave his homeland, family ties, and familiar surroundings to head into an unknown land, Canaan, Abraham did not hesitate. He took only his wife, Sarah, and his nephew, Lot, and embarked on this daunting journey. This was not merely a physical relocation; it was a deep act of spiritual surrender. Abraham packed up his entire life, possessions included, and chose to trust God's plan, believing in the incredible promise that his descendants would become a great nation.

As the years unfolded, Abraham's faith was assessed repeatedly. Despite the passage of time and the lack of a child, he clung to the promises of the Lord. His struggles are relatable; at times, he and Sarah faced discouragement and made decisions that were less than wise. Yet, through it all, their faith endured. At the age of 90, Sarah finally gave birth to Isaac, with Abraham being 100 at the time—an event that seemed impossible, yet it was a testament to God's perfect timing. Their story emphasizes that faith is not a sprint but a marathon; perseverance in belief is crucial, even in the face of discouragement.

Has God ever nudged you towards something that felt uncomfortable or even impossible? Did you surrender your desires and step out in faith, just like Noah and Abraham? It is important to remember, especially during moments of uncertainty, the patience demonstrated by Abraham. His faith did not waver over the years. God has not promised us an easy life, but rather, He has assured us of His unfailing love and faithfulness.

When we are faced with challenges and may not see immediate results, we should think of Noah's resolve and Abraham's long wait for the fulfillment of God's promise. We must trust and surrender our wills to Him. In doing this, we can finally rest with reassurance that God will take care of the rest. In doing so, we can rest assured that God will take care of the rest. His plans unfold in His timing, which is always perfect.

Surrender Releases the Past

"Forget the former things; do not dwell on the past."
(Isaiah 43:18).

To walk confidently with God, I first had to forgive myself and release the shame of my past. That healing did not come overnight. It took the steady work of the twelve steps, the guidance of counseling, and daily time in God's presence. Little by little, I learned how to move forward instead of staying bound to regret.

When I finally surrendered everything to Him, God began to redeem what I thought disqualified me. The path was not easy; it required time, persistence, and complete trust. But as I released my past, God transformed it into purpose. He began sending women into my life who carried the same burdens of alcoholism, infidelity, and shame that I once did, and I was able to walk beside them with compassion and hope.

I saw the miracles unfolding in their lives, just as I had experienced on my own. In that moment, I realized God was redeeming my past, reshaping it into something beautiful, and calling me to share my story. In Him, I had been given a new identity.

Every believer faces a pivotal moment of decision: Will we continue to drag our past behind us like a heavy chain, or will we lay it at the feet of Jesus and walk in freedom? For a long time, I clung to shame, regret, addiction, and heartbreak because they felt familiar. However, the longer I held on, the more they weighed me down. Only when I truly surrendered my past to God did I begin to experience real healing. Scripture tells us in 2 Corinthians 5:17: "If anyone is in Christ, he is a new creation. The old has passed away; behold, the new has come." That is not just poetic language; it is a promise.

Letting go of the past does not mean pretending it did not happen. It involves acknowledging it, bringing it before the Lord, and trusting Him to redeem it. There are parts of my story that I once wished to erase, but now I see them as evidence of God's grace. Romans 8:28 reminds us that "in all things, God works for the good of those who love him, who have been called according to his purpose." This means that even the messes and the moments we wish we could take back, He can use them. He wastes nothing.

Fear of judgment and the belief that God could forgive others but not me stalled my surrender for so long. But that is not who God is. Psalm 103:12 says, "As far as the east is from the west, so far has he removed our transgressions from us." That is an infinite distance. That is grace. When God forgives, He does not hold it over our heads or keep score; He sets us free.

Surrender is a daily act. It is not a one-time prayer; it is a lifestyle. Each day, I must choose to believe what God says about me over what the enemy whispers. I need to trust that my identity is not rooted in who I am alone, but in who I am in Christ. Galatians 2:20 states, "I have been crucified with Christ. It is no longer I who live, but Christ who lives in me." I rely on this truth when my past tries to creep back in.

> **Surrender is a daily act.**

If you are still holding on to your past, let me encourage you to give it to God, all of it. The guilt, the wounds, the stories you have never told, lay them down. He already knows, and He loves you anyway. There is freedom on the other side of surrender. There is healing, a purpose, and most importantly, there is a Savior who is unafraid of your past, He desires your heart.

Surrender Recognizes Our Blessings and Our Battles

I began dating my husband in 2015. After our first date, we both knew marriage would be our next step. The following year, we wed. Then came our son Grant, one year later.

My family is my greatest blessing. I prayed for a child for ten years, and God, in His perfect timing, answered that prayer in 2016. But parenting is not without its challenges. At the beginning of first grade, my son began to shut down. We tried everything—punishment, positive reinforcement, rewards—but nothing worked. Then finally, I prayed. Why had I not done this sooner? Instead I had relied on my fifteen years of teaching experience and my maternal instincts, believing they were enough. I had forgotten to pray. Gosh, how often do we all do this!

Sometimes, our greatest blessings also bring the greatest challenges. But when I finally turned to God, I received the direction I desperately needed. We sought professional help, made a conscious effort to model good behavior at home, and, most importantly, I prayed every morning. I surrendered Grant to God, asking for guidance, patience, and wisdom. Over time, he began to thrive. Through this trial, God taught me many lessons, but the most important one was to surrender my family to Him in prayer.

Praying over our family should not be our last resort, it should be our first response. As parents, spouses, siblings, and children, we have the privilege of lifting our loved ones to God daily. Pray for your children's protection, that God would guard their hearts and minds. Pray for your spouse, that your marriage would be strengthened and centered on Christ. Ask for wisdom in parenting, patience in conflict, and grace in daily interactions. Speak blessings over your home, inviting God's presence into every room. If your child is struggling, pray for peace, clarity, and perseverance. If your family is facing trials, ask God to be your refuge and strength.

When we pray over our loved ones, we release control and place them in the hands of the One who loves them even more than we do.

Surrender Resists the Urge to Control

It is one thing to hand God our struggles when life feels out of control—illness, infertility, financial hardship, or career uncertainty. But what about the moments when we try to hold the reins ourselves? The truth is, surrender often resists our deepest instinct: the urge to control outcomes, manipulate circumstances, or cling to the illusion that we are in charge. Yet control is a counterfeit comfort. It promises peace but delivers exhaustion.

Scripture reminds us that surrender is stronger than control. Proverbs 3:5–6 tells us, "Trust in the Lord with all your heart and lean not on your own understanding; in all your ways submit to him, and he will make your paths straight." Trusting God brings a peace that surpasses all understanding, requiring us to loosen our grip on our own knowledge and submit to His wisdom instead.

King David models this release beautifully. He begins by acknowledging his dependence on God: "Keep me safe, O God, for I have come to you for refuge" (Psalm 16:1).

Then he resists the temptation to take credit for his blessings: "I said to the Lord, 'You are my Master! Every good thing I have comes from you." (Psalm 16:2). Finally, David surrenders completely: "I know the Lord is always with me. I will not be shaken, for he is right beside me." (Psalm 16:8–9). David's example shows us that true surrender does not just release pain; it resists the very human urge to control. It steadies us in trust, anchors us in gratitude, and liberates us to rest in God's presence instead of striving to manage everything ourselves.

When we resist the urge to control and instead surrender our struggles, fears, and uncertainties to God, peace follows. We no longer carry the burden alone; our Heavenly Father takes the weight, walking beside us every step of the way. Just as David declared, "I will not be shaken, for he is right beside me" (Psalm 16:8). The truth is, we are never left to navigate life's challenges by ourselves. The Holy Spirit, our constant companion, is always present—we only need to call on Him.

God never promised us a life free from hardship, sorrow, or uncertainty, but He did promise His presence amid it. This is a promise that brings hope and encouragement. Control demands answers and guarantees; surrender rests in God's faithfulness. When we release not only our fears and insecurities but also our blessings into His hands, we find the peace that control can never provide. And here is the hope: God always responds. Sometimes His answer comes swiftly, other times slowly, but always with perfect timing. The surest path to peace is found not in grasping tighter, but in full surrender.

Surrender also involves acceptance. In those first months of sobriety, I found myself clinging to a familiar prayer from recovery circles. It reminded me to release what I could not control, take courageous steps where I could, and trust God for the wisdom to know the difference. I repeated those truths until they took root in my heart, and God began to steady me in places that once felt impossible to navigate.

This simple yet profound prayer became a daily anchor, reminding me that true surrender is not about passively giving up, but about actively trusting God with what is beyond my control. It taught me that acceptance is not resignation, it is faith in action. By acknowledging the things we cannot change, we release them into God's hands, allowing Him to work in His perfect way and timing.

Principles That Anchored My Recovery

- **Acceptance:** Trusting God's sovereignty over what I cannot control (Philippians 4:6–7).

- **Courage:** Taking bold, obedient steps where change is possible (Joshua 1:9).

- **Wisdom:** Seeking discernment to know the difference between surrender and responsibility (James 1:5).

- **Surrender:** Letting go of outcomes and resting in God's will and timing (Proverbs 3:5–6).

These practices reshaped my recovery, grounding me in God's truth and guiding me into lasting peace and freedom.

Early in my journey, I was told something that has stuck with me: *You cannot change people, places, or things. The only thing you can profoundly change is yourself.* That realization was both humbling and freeing. I had spent so much time trying to control circumstances and fix others, only to end up frustrated and exhausted. But the moment I shifted my focus inward, choosing to change my own heart, mindset, and actions, I found true transformation.

Changing another person is impossible—only God can transform lives. I am living proof of this truth. For nineteen years, I battled addiction, trapped in a cycle that no human intervention could break. No amount of pleading, reasoning, or effort from others could relieve my alcoholism or heal the deep-seated desires that kept me bound. It was only when I admitted my weakness and surrendered to the Holy Spirit that real change began to occur.

Every day, I witness heartbreaking stories of families struggling with a loved one lost in addiction. Husbands, wives, and children desperately hope and pray for their loved ones to break free. You cannot force someone to change; the desire for transformation must come from within. The person with an addiction must first recognize their need for change and ultimately surrender to God's power. This principle extends beyond addiction—whether it involves weight loss, smoking, financial struggles, or any other personal battle, genuine change begins within. We are all responsible for our choices, but real and lasting change happens when we place our trust in God's grace, follow His guidance, and act. Change cannot take place without desire and action.

Sometimes, we yearn for a change of location, but God has a different plan that requires trust and surrender. He opens doors in His own time, not ours. In recovery, there is a saying: "You can move to another city, but you are taking the problem with you… you." This truth extends beyond addiction; it serves as a reminder that external changes do not resolve internal struggles. Instead of constantly looking ahead to unfamiliar places, opportunities, or chapters, we must learn to be present where God has placed us.

As I reflect on this, I remind myself of this lesson. Too often, I worry about tomorrow and lose sight of today, forgetting that God's plan is unfolding right where I am. While I may not always be able to change my location, I can change my perspective. Surrendering to His will means embracing the present, seeking growth opportunities, and serving with gratitude in the place He has called me to be.

Sometimes, we desperately want to change certain things in our lives. We long for circumstances to shift quickly and drastically. But often, that is not God's plan. Instead, He calls us to wait. We pray and seek, yet the situation remains the same. In these moments, God reassures us of His presence, sending reminders that He is with us. I find myself in such a season now. A friend reaches out daily, saying, "God put you on my heart this morning. I am praying for you." Or "I felt led to call and remind you that you are not alone." These messages bring comfort, yet the change I long for has not come. And so, I wait.

Waiting is never easy, but Scripture reminds us it is a time of growth and trust. Isaiah 40:31 declares, "But those who wait on the Lord shall renew their strength; they shall mount up with wings like eagles; they shall run and not be weary; they shall walk and not faint." God's timing is perfect, even when it is not what we anticipated. Proverbs 3:5-6 urges us to "Trust in the Lord with all your heart and lean not on your understanding; in all your ways submit to Him, and He will make your paths straight." I cannot change my current situation, only God can. My role is not to force a solution but to surrender fully, trusting that His plans are more significant than mine. So, I wait, knowing that in the waiting, He is working, refining me, and preparing the path ahead. All we must do is surrender.

Surrender is not a one-time decision; it is a daily practice. We step into a life of greater peace, purpose, and freedom when we release our need for control and trust in God's sovereignty. It does not mean our struggles disappear; we no longer face them alone. We must let go of our worries, fears, and desires each day, trusting that God's plan is better than our own. True surrender is not about losing—it is about gaining the strength, wisdom, and peace that only He can provide.

Surrender Transforms Struggle Into Strength

"Cast your cares on the Lord and he will sustain you; he will never let the righteous be shaken" (Psalm 55:22).

Surrender is not a one-time decision, but a lifestyle we must adopt. Even when we voice to God, "I'm surrendering this to You," our reflex is to step back in and try to control the outcome. This tension is an integral part of our humanity. However, peace takes root when we release our grip and allow God to perform what only He can. One powerful way to surrender is to say it aloud: "God, I am giving this to you. You know best. Not me. Guide me. Open the doors that need opening. Close the ones that need closing. Keep me on the right path and give me all the resources I need."

When I struggled with lingering resentment one summer, I brought it to God, but it did not disappear. It was not until I admitted it to my friend Amy, prayed aloud, and continued to pray daily, that I began to heal. Saying it aloud took the power away from the enemy and returned it to God.

Another helpful tool is journaling the areas of your life you are still holding onto, those places that are hardest to surrender. As you write, invite God into those pages and trust His sovereignty to do what you cannot.

Ask yourself:

- Am I holding on to resentment?

- Is something replacing my time with God?

- Share your thoughts with a trusted friend or mentor.

Confession brings clarity. Surrender brings freedom.

Do Not Manipulate

"All you need to say is simply 'Yes' or 'No;' anything beyond this comes from the evil one." (Matthew 5:37).

Manipulation often hides in the small stuff. I learned this firsthand in my marriage. I used to barter my emotions: "If you do this, then I'll do that." My husband, West, saw through it and lovingly called it out. And honestly? He was right.

Manipulation is sneaky. It shows up in guilt trips, selective truths, and withheld affection. Sometimes we use kindness as currency, expecting something in return. But when love is transactional, it is no longer unconditional.

Psychologist David Buss and his research team conducted a widely respected study that broke manipulation down into six main strategies people use to get their way.

These include:

- **Charm** – using praise or flattery to win someone over.

- **Reason** – persuading through logic or carefully chosen arguments.

- **Coercion** – pushing, pressuring, or intimidating someone into agreement.

- **Silent treatment** – shutting down communication to punish or control.

- **Regression** – acting helpless, pouting, or reverting to childish behavior to influence others.

- **Debasement** – putting yourself down to gain sympathy or compliance.

The study also found that charm is typically used to start or influence behavior, while tactics like coercion and silent treatment are used to stop or control it.[1]

These tactics are not just found in research, they show up in our everyday lives, often in subtle ways we do not recognize in ourselves until the Holy Spirit holds up a mirror. One time I downplayed the cost of a sofa, calling it "about $700" when it was $799.99. That is a lie by omission. Why did I do it? Fear. Fear that if I told the whole truth, I would not get what I wanted. But God sees the heart. And He wants ours surrendered.

---

1 David M. Buss, Mary Gomes, Dolly S. Higgins, and Karen Lauterbach, "Tactics of Manipulation," *Journal of Personality and Social Psychology* 52, no. 6 (June 1987): 1219-29, https://doi. org/10.1037/0022-3514.52.6.1219

Even biblical heroes fell into manipulation. Adam blamed Eve. Eve blamed the serpent. The result? Consequences that echo through history.

"You will desire to control your husband, but he will rule over you" (Genesis 3:16).

That desire to control did not start with us, it started in Eden. But freedom begins when we stop the cycle. When we hand God the keys, He drives us toward peace.

Do Not Complain

"Do everything without grumbling or arguing...Then you will shine among them like stars in the sky." (Philippians 2:14-15).

I married a good man. He follows Jesus, works hard, and serves our family faithfully. And yet, I catch myself complaining because he does not affirm me in the exact way I want. Why? Because I am human. And humans complain.

Even the Apostle Paul, writing from prison, reminded the church to do all things without complaining. If Paul could rejoice while locked up, I could probably make it through a Monday without grumbling over my coffee spill.

Why We Complain:

- Emotional release (venting to feel heard)

- Social bonding (misery loves company)

- Attention-seeking (seeking validation)

- Negative bias (our brains fixate on the bad)

- Powerlessness (a cry for help)

But when complaining becomes constant, it poisons our perspective. If we do not surrender our frustrations, we start to identify with them.

How to Stop the Spiral:

- Practice daily gratitude.

- Pinpoint your root complaint: what is *really* bothering you?

- Pray before you speak.

- Focus on solutions, not just the problems.

- Speak to someone who can help (not just someone who will agree).

When our mouths praise instead of pout, we look more like Jesus and less like the world. Gratitude is the antidote to complaint. It is a weapon against the enemy's lies.

Do Not Compare

"I praise you because I am fearfully and wonderfully made; your works are wonderful; I know that full well." (Psalm 139:14).

Scrolling through social media can steal your peace in thirty seconds flat. One minute, I am content. Next, I am wondering why my husband did not post a love letter on Instagram.

But love is not found in highlight reels. It is on Sunday night trash runs, folded laundry, and the way he holds my hand during the sermon. That is the real stuff. The stuff comparison hides.

Why We Compare:

- Self-evaluation (am I enough?)

- Motivation (can I do better?)

- Social pressure (am I keeping up?)

The Dangers:

- Dissatisfaction

- Insecurity

- Negative self-talk

Social media is a showroom of polished exteriors. But God sees our hearts. He is not comparing your Tuesday to someone else's curated Friday night. He made you for a purpose, and His plan is custom designed.

How to Break the Comparison Trap:

- Create a gratitude list when envy strikes

- Memorize identity-affirming scriptures like:

  1. Genesis 1:27 "God created mankind in His own image..."

  2. Ephesians 2:10 "We are God's handiwork..."

- Reflect on how God uniquely wired you

- Ask: Who am I trying to impress, and why?

Comparison steals contentment. But gratitude restores it. When we trust God's timing and design, we realize we do not need to compare our journey to anyone else's. Surrender invites us to stop striving for someone else's finish line and start walking faithfully in our own lane. It is saying, "God, I release the pressure to measure up. I trust You with my timeline, my gifts, and even my pace." When we surrender the need to compete or compare, we begin to walk in peace, no longer striving for worth but resting in the truth that we are already deeply known and fully loved. That is where freedom begins.

Surrender in this area is not easy, it rubs against our pride, our timelines, and our desire to be seen. But what if the very things we envy in others are the things God never intended for us to carry? What if peace is not found in catching up, but in slowing down long enough to hear Him say, "You are exactly where I want you?" Letting go of comparison is an act of trust, trusting that your life is unfolding under the watchful eye of a good and faithful God. And that trust, that is where surrender takes root and grows.

Surrendering the compass of our lives is not a one-time activity, but a lifelong journey of releasing, trusting, and choosing peace over control. Whether it is our daily decisions, deep-rooted fears, past regrets, or even our most cherished blessings, God calls us to lay it all at His feet. True surrender does not strip us of strength, it refines it. It transforms our struggles into testimonies and our control into Christ-centered clarity. As we let go of manipulation, complaints, and comparison, we make space for joy, intimacy with God, and deep, lasting freedom. So today, hold the compass loosely. You were never meant to steer this ship alone. The One who calms storms is already at the helm. Let Him lead.

When we finally loosen our grip on the compass, we can pray the words that steady our course and surrender the journey to the One who knows the way. It was in that season that I began surrendering my will to God in a deeper way, trusting Him to reshape my desires, reorder my steps, and free me from patterns I could not break on my own.

Guided by Prayer

Prayer is the GPS, Not the Spare Tire

"Prayer is simply the key to everything we need to do and be in life."

—Timothy Keller

August 2013

This was no ordinary morning; it was my first day back at work after leaving for rehab. For six years, I had taught high school history at my alma mater, but the school year had started two weeks earlier without me. In a town like ours, where everyone knows everything, my absence had already sparked assumptions and whispers. To make matters worse, my classroom was right next door to my soon-to-be ex-husband's. The weight of shame, anxiety, and dread pressed down hard. If ever there was a morning I needed peace, it was this one.

So, before I faced the day, I sat on the patio of my new apartment, one hand wrapped around a warm cup of coffee, the other holding my daily devotion. The Alabama morning was already thick with heat, but that did not stop me from turning to God. I took a deep breath, flipped to the day's page, and bowed my head. My mind was swirling with worry, so I kept it simple. I prayed:

"God, be with me in every way today. Please give me the strength to face whatever comes. Help me feel Your presence in each moment and hold my head high, because I know the Holy Spirit walks with me. I am a miracle. Please help me keep going, even when fear and anxiety try to sneak in. Show me how to serve others, even in my healing. Amen."

That whisper of prayer did not change my circumstances, but it shifted my soul. It reminded me that I was not alone. That sacred moment on the patio became my lifeline, my anchor. Since then, I have discovered something powerful: when we pray not only in crisis but also in the everyday moments of life. We begin to experience a peace that defies explanation.

Prayer does not require perfection. You do not need to speak in eloquent sentences or know all the right words; you just need to speak from the heart. Close your eyes, take a deep breath, and talk to God, it is that simple. However, making prayer a daily practice requires intention. Spiritual maturity does not happen overnight; it progresses through small, faithful choices. Each prayer, each act of trust, becomes a step in that journey of growth. Over time, those choices change how we perceive everything.

Daily prayers and complete surrender to God go hand in hand. Real peace comes when we release our fears to God and continue to talk to Him as we walk through them. We can pray over our worries, our children, our workdays, our grief, and our gratitude; nothing is too small or too messy for God. When we pray along the way, we invite Him into every part of our journey.

Morning Prayers

Starting my day with prayer has become a vital part of my routine. I begin with a short devotion and then move into focused prayer. To stay centered, I keep a prayer list on my phone. It reminds me to be intentional, to pause, to lift names and needs, to remember that my time with God is sacred.

Here is a sample of one of the morning prayers I keep saved on my phone:

- Thank you, Lord, for everything you have given me.

- Please help me serve you today.

- Please show me what I need to focus on today.

- Help me stop rushing through my day.

- Take away my doubt and fear.

- Please help me avoid becoming angry or resentful.

- Please grant love, peace, and joy to _________________. (List the person I am struggling to like during this season.)

- Please help me be satisfied and grateful.

- Teach me to live in the moment.

- Please bless my husband, my son, my daughter, my parents, and my mother-in-law.

Then, I add the names of others who need prayer that week. Sometimes I sit in silence. I meditate on Scripture or reflect on a word or thought God placed on my heart. Sometimes I sit with the goodness of God. Other times, I wait for Him to speak. I ask for guidance and clarity, and I try to listen, even when the answer is "wait." Waiting does not come easily to me, but prayer teaches patience.

Prayer is not just a habit; it is my daily oxygen. Recently, I spoke with friends in recovery who had relapsed. Every single one of them said the first thing they stopped doing was praying. That hit me hard. What may seem like a small practice, just a few minutes each morning, is what holds us together. Prayer keeps us grounded in God, not ourselves. It is the difference between striving and surrendering.

Morning prayer is more than a routine; it is a lifeline. It centers our hearts, aligns our thoughts, and arms us for whatever the day brings. When we begin each morning in God's presence, we experience the kind of peace that carries us forward. We remember we are not doing this life alone. Whatever comes, we have already prayed our way into the day, and God is walking every step beside us.

Gratitude Prayers

When I got sober eleven years ago, a spiritual awakening changed everything for me. As I opened my eyes to Christ and embraced His plan for my life, I realized how distorted my view of spirituality had been. For over three decades, I treated God like a genie, approaching Him with a list of wants rather than a heart of worship. I prayed only when I needed something, rarely taking the time to thank Him or to ask how I could serve Him. Gratitude was not just absent; it felt foreign.

Everything changed when I made gratitude a daily practice. My life regained color and clarity. I became intensely aware of the blessings around me. During treatment, I realized how much I had to be thankful for. Many of the women with me had no home, no job, and no family to return to, while I had all three. That realization became the foundation of my gratitude.

Each morning, I wrote down three things for which I was thankful. With every entry, the Holy Spirit warmed my soul. I stopped taking things for granted and began to see God's hand in everything. His grace had saved my life. As I leaned into His presence, miracles began to multiply. I recorded both the significant blessings, like restored relationships, and the smaller ones, like learning to sleep without fear.

That journal became my testimony. Page after page told the story of God's faithfulness. Gratitude transformed my prayer life and renewed my mind. Science confirms what I experienced: practicing gratitude activates the brain's reward system, releasing dopamine and serotonin—chemicals responsible for joy and emotional well-being.[2] In one study, individuals who kept gratitude journals reported higher optimism, stronger physical health, and fewer doctor visits than those who focused on daily stressors.[3]

Gratitude is not just a mood booster; it is brain changing. It rewires us to see beauty, expect good, and connect deeply with others. MRI scans reveal that gratitude strengthens neural pathways associated with empathy, morality, and emotional awareness. Gratitude does not just lift our hearts—it transforms our brains and our lives.[4]

Prayers of gratitude became the heartbeat of my recovery. I stopped begging God for more and started thanking Him for what I already had. The words did not need to be poetic—just honest: "Thank You for my home. Thank You for my health. Thank You for today." Over time, those simple prayers reshaped my thinking.

2 Roland Zahn et al., "The Neural Basis of Human Social Values: Evidence from Functional MRI," *Cerebral Cortex* 19, no. 2 (2009): 276–83, https://doi.org/10.1093/cercor/bhn080.

3 Robert A. Emmons and Michael E. McCullough, "Counting Blessings versus Burdens: An Experimental Investigation of Gratitude and Subjective Well-Being in Daily Life," *Journal of Personality and Social Psychology* 84, no. 2 (2003): 377–89.

4 Gregory R. Fox et al., "Neural Correlates of Gratitude," *Frontiers in Psychology* 6 (2015): 1491, https://doi.org/10.3389/fpsyg.2015.01491.

Scripture emphasizes this repeatedly:

> "Give thanks in all circumstances; for this is God's will for you in Christ Jesus." (1 Thessalonians 5:18).

> "Enter his gates with thanksgiving and his courts with praise; give thanks to him and praise his name." (Psalms 100:4).

These verses are not mere suggestions; they are sacred invitations to draw closer to God. Gratitude opens the door to His presence. It changes our perspective on what surrounds us and deepens our trust in who He is: faithful, generous, and endlessly patient. Today, my gratitude is not based on perfection; it is rooted in His presence. And His presence changes everything.

Prayer, the Gift That Keeps Giving

Prayers of gratitude help shape our inner world, but prayer itself consistently, honest, heart-driven prayer—has an impact far beyond our soul. It transforms everything. For Christians, prayer is not optional; it is essential. It is the bridge between us and God's presence, the connection that steadies us in chaos and anchors us in love.

Modern science confirms what the Bible has been saying for centuries: prayer not only changes our hearts but also our bodies. Medical studies have found that consistent prayer can:

- Lower blood pressure

- Decrease heart rate

- Reduce stress and anxiety

- Increase melatonin and serotonin levels

- Strengthening the immune system

- Diminish pain or increase pain tolerance

- Improve mood

- Elevate self-esteem

When we pray through life's joys, stresses, quiet mornings, and sleepless nights, we invite God into our biology, our emotions, and our very being.[5] We not only survive hard days, but they sustain us.[6]

One place I especially turn to prayer is at night. Sleep often eludes me. My mind races through the day's regrets or tomorrow's to-do list. But when I lie in bed and pray, really pray, I feel my breathing slow and my spirit quiet. I begin by thanking God for the day: the good, the hard, the growth. Then I name my worries, lifting each one like a child handing over broken toys to a parent who knows how to fix them. Peace does not always come instantly, but it always comes.

Scientific studies support this nighttime rhythm of prayer. Researchers at the University of Rochester Medical Center found that prayer and meditation activate areas of the brain associated with emotional regulation, empathy, and self-awareness—traits that directly impact our sleep and relationships. When we practice prayer consistently, it reshapes our response to life's pressures.[7]

I love it when science backs up Scripture, don't you? The Bible has been teaching us all along that prayer changes everything. It realigns our focus, strengthens our faith, and soothes our nervous

---

5 Chittaranjan Andrade and Rajiv Radhakrishnan, "Prayer and Healing: A Medical and Scientific Perspective on Randomized Controlled Trials," *Indian Journal of Psychiatry* 51, no. 4 (2009): 247–53, https://www.ncbi.nlm.nih.gov/pmc/articles/PMC2802370/.

6 Jeff Levin, "How Faith Heals: A Theoretical Model," *Explore* 5, no. 2 (2009): 77–96, https://www.ncbi.nlm.nih.gov/pmc/articles/PMC2654362/.

7 Andrew Newberg and Mark Robert Waldman, *How God Changes Your Brain: Breakthrough Findings from a Leading Neuroscientist* (New York: Ballantine Books, 2009).

system. Prayer, especially when paired with gratitude, renews our minds and helps us press forward with hope. We begin each morning with prayer, end each night by surrendering in prayer, and stay grounded, grateful, and growing through prayer all along the way.

Praying the Armor of God

Prayer is more than just a source of comfort; it is our armor. It prepares us for the spiritual battles we face daily, both seen and unseen. In Ephesians 6, the Apostle Paul urges believers to "put on the full armor of God" so we can stand firm against evil. However, this armor is incomplete without prayer. Prayer is the thread that ties every piece together and the power that activates each defense.

Paul writes,

"Therefore put on the whole armor of God, so that when the day of evil comes, you may be able to stand your ground, … And pray in the Spirit on all occasions with all kinds of prayers and requests. …be alert and always keep on praying for all the Lord's people." (Ephesians 6:13, 18).

This is not merely a suggestion; it is a strategy. Paul understood that we are engaged in a constant battle—not just with our circumstances but also with lies, shame, comparison, and doubt. Prayer is our way to fight back.

Each piece of armor protects various aspects of us: the belt of truth grounds us, the breastplate of righteousness guards our hearts, the shield of faith extinguishes the flaming lies, the helmet of salvation secures our identity, and the sword of the Spirit, which is God's Word, serves as our weapon. None of these pieces function fully without prayer. Prayer is what activates our armor. Without it, we may know God's truth but forget to live it out.

For me, prayer serves as my daily defense against insecurity. Occasionally I wake up hearing thoughts like:

- I am not good enough.

- I am not well-liked.

- I do not know the Bible well enough to teach it.

- I should have managed that better.

You may have had mornings like that too, when the enemy starts whispering doubts even before your feet hit the floor. That is when I pray. I say, "Lord, remind me who I am in You." I ask Him to replace lies with truth and to help me walk not in perfection, but in purpose. Some days, peace comes quickly; on other days, I must continue praying through it. Each prayer is part of the armor I put on.

When peace does not come immediately, I write down the lies I am battling and ask, "What does God's Word say instead?" I stay in conversation with God, and sometimes I reach out to a trusted friend to pray with me. Often, that is when a breakthrough occurs. When we pray along the way, we do not just put on armor; we actively walk in it.

Here is what I have learned: Resistance often means you are on the right path. The more the enemy pushes, the more confident I am that the Holy Spirit is at work. So, I keep praying. I put on the armor. And I keep moving forward.

> **Prayer is not a backup plan; it's a first move.**

Prayer is not a backup plan; it's a first move. It provides clarity when confusion clouds our minds and steadies us when fear tries to shake our faith. When you start your day by *praying* on the armor of God, you leave your home not just protected but empowered.

And when the battle comes, you will not be caught empty-handed. You will be grounded in truth, covered in peace, and equipped with prayer. You are ready to stand firm.

The Serenity Prayer

The Serenity Prayer is most attributed to theologian Reinhold Niebuhr, though its exact origins remain debated. Regardless of who penned it, it holds eternal truth. Its quiet strength has anchored recovery communities for decades, comforted grieving hearts, and reminded millions to surrender what is out of their hands.[8]

The first time I prayed this prayer was at a twelve-step meeting during rehab. I glanced around the room at the other patients, strangers to me, yet familiar in their brokenness. Their weary faces, their subtle nods, told me what words could not: we were more alike than different. Each of us was stumbling through the rubble of our lives, desperate for something real. As we spoke the prayer aloud together, the Holy Spirit settled over the room like a quiet weight of peace. Some walked away that day changed, others not.

It was through that simple prayer of surrender that I first began to understand what yielding my will to God really meant. It did not feel like a formula or a church saying, it felt like oxygen when I could not breathe on my own. In those early days of recovery, each line invited me to trust God with what I could not control, to find courage when obedience cost something, and to seek wisdom when I did not know the way forward. As I began not just to say it but to live it, something in me started to change. Life did not get easier, but my heart got softer, steadier, and anchored. One truth stood out clearly: this prayer only had power if I chose to live it.

---

8 Reinhold Niebuhr, *The Serenity Prayer, in The Essential Reinhold Niebuhr: Selected Essays and Addresses*, ed. Robert McAfee Brown (New Haven, CT: Yale University Press, 1986), 251.

I began praying for the people I resented and the people I had hurt. I asked God to soften their hearts, but first—He softened mine. I begged Him to take away the craving for alcohol, to clear the fog in my mind, and to give me the strength to walk through each hard step of recovery with both grit and grace. Some prayers were whispered. Some were angry. Some were nothing but tears. I did not know if God would fix my life, but I was finally asking Him to have it—all of it.

This was not polished faith. It was raw surrender. No fancy words, no perfect theology—just a desperate girl talking to a patient God. And that is where the shift happened. Not when life got better, but when my heart finally bowed. Because prayer only became powerful when I stopped reciting it…and started living it.

Change did not come in dramatic flashes. It emerged slowly, in daily prayers, whispered through fear, and spoken through trembling faith. It came when I was sitting at my desk, overwhelmed by the life I was rebuilding, and I reached for the one thing that always brought me clarity: prayer. Sometimes I wrote the Serenity Prayer down repeatedly, each line reminding me who holds absolute control. Prayer became my path through life's most challenging seasons.

In times of transition or trauma, it is not just a routine, it is your compass and guide. At first, it may feel almost too simple, but when every other option fails, you discover it is the most powerful thing you can do.

Prayer is the place where surrender takes root. Scripture shows us that prayer is where we lay down our understanding and trust God's leading (Proverbs 3:5–6). Through prayer, He gives peace in what we cannot control, courage to take the steps we must, and wisdom to discern the difference. I learned that surrender is not just a verse or a concept, it is a daily posture before a faithful God, one that begins in honest conversation with Him.

What started as a prayer someone handed me in rehab became something much more personal. Recovery brought me back to

God, but it did not teach me how to stay with Him. I had to choose that on my own. I learned that no one else could say my prayers for me. I needed quiet—just me and God—to wrestle, confess, listen, and breathe. That is where real surrender began to deepen. Not in a meeting, not in a script, but in the everyday rhythm of seeking Him, before the day unraveled, before the world got loud. The power was never in the prayer itself, but in the God who met me there, again and again.

Praying for Loved Ones

"Therefore, confess your sins to each other and pray for each other so that you may be healed. The prayer of a righteous person is powerful and effective." (James 5:16).

Prayer does not merely sustain us; it also flows outward, blessing the lives of those around us. When we pray for our loved ones, we participate in God's work of healing, protection, and transformation. Interceding in prayer is one of the most powerful ways we can show love to someone.

I learned this lesson unexpectedly during my time in graduate school when I started attending a charismatic Church of God congregation, which was quite different from my Southern Baptist roots. On one of my first Sundays, while sitting in the choir loft, the man next to me began speaking in tongues. I remember thinking, "What have I gotten myself into?" However, as time went on, I became more comfortable. One evening, at a youth conference, a fellow volunteer pulled me aside and told me, "While I was praying, God revealed to me that your spiritual gift is prayer." I have never forgotten those words.

In the initial stages of my sobriety, I had little to offer emotionally or financially. I was in the process of rebuilding my life. However, I had one gift I could offer freely: prayer. I began praying regularly for the people God placed in my life—family, friends, mentors, and even strangers. Something shifted in me.

As I prayed for others, my heart changed. My compassion deepened, and my empathy grew. Prayer gave me the ability to see beyond myself and the courage to believe that God could work powerfully in someone else's life.

Paul writes in 1 Timothy 2:1, "I urge, then, first of all, that petitions, prayers, intercessions, and thanksgivings be made for all people." This call is broad, but it often begins with those we love most. As we pray for them, we also grow in grace. Interceding trains our hearts to trust God's timing, surrender our control, and anchor others in the presence of the One who knows them best.

Whether your loved ones are facing illness, heartache, addiction, or simply the weight of everyday life, your prayers matter. Even when you cannot fix a problem or change an outcome, you can lift it up to the One who can. As you pray, you not only know that God hears you, but you begin to see that He is also at work on your behalf.

Praying for others is not just a ministry; it is a form of discipleship. It aligns your heart with God's and teaches you to love without limits. So, when someone comes to mind, do not just think of them; pray for them. Your prayer may be the very thing God uses to change everything.

Praying Through Obstacles in Life

Life does not provide us with a roadmap. We encounter twists, setbacks, and unexpected storms. But here is the good news: we do not have to face these challenges alone. Prayer is how we navigate through chaos without losing hope. It is how we hold God's hand when the road gets rough. Prayer is meant to be our GPS, guiding us step by step, not the spare tire we reach for only when everything has already fallen apart. It keeps us aligned with God's direction, steadying our hearts before the detours and breakdowns come. When prayer becomes our guide rather than our last resort, we discover peace even in the middle of life's storms.

Obstacles come in many forms—financial pressure, strained relationships, career changes, parenting struggles, chronic illness, grief, and spiritual dryness. Sometimes we juggle too much, while other times, it is God's silence that is the hardest to bear. In all these moments, prayer is our pathway to peace.

Philippians 4:6–7 invites us:

> "Do not be anxious about anything, but in every situation, by prayer and petition, with thanksgiving, present your requests to God. And the peace of God, which transcends all understanding, will guard your hearts and your minds in Christ Jesus."

This verse is not just a reminder for your refrigerator; it is a strategy for your soul. God is not asking us to ignore our anxiety; He invites us to bring it all to Him. When we pray through the chaos, confusion, and daily unknowns, we position ourselves to receive a peace the world cannot explain.

Isaiah 41:10 provides another powerful reminder:

> "Fear not, for I am with you; be not dismayed, for I am your God; I will strengthen you, I will help you, I will uphold you with my righteous right hand."

In moments when your world feels upside down, when you have lost a job, received a difficult diagnosis, or said goodbye to someone you love, it is here that prayer does its deepest work. It may not erase the pain, but it anchors you in the presence of the One who never leaves.

Many of our most challenging battles are internal: the disappointment of unfulfilled dreams, the sting of failure, the temptation to compare ourselves to others, and the ache of wondering if our lives truly matter. In these hidden struggles, prayer realigns our identity. It helps us hear God's voice above the lies and keeps us grounded when everything else is shifting.

I have found that when I pray over my pain, rather than letting it fester in silence, God speaks to me. Perhaps not in the way I expect, but always in the way I need. Sometimes He gives peace. Sometimes He provides the next step. But He always reveals Himself.

Praying through obstacles does not mean we ignore them; it means we acknowledge them and face them with faith. We stop pretending we are okay and start trusting the One who is in control. As we pray, the burden becomes lighter, not because life is easy, but because we are not carrying it alone.

So, if you are facing something challenging today, start with a prayer. It does not have to be elaborate; it just needs to be genuine. God is not waiting for perfection; He is waiting for your invitation into your circumstance. Let prayer be the path that carries you to a peaceful situation.

Praying Over Your Goals and Dreams

Each of us carries dreams tucked quietly into the corners of our hearts and others boldly displayed on vision boards. Your dream might be to author a book, start a family, launch a ministry, establish a business, or live a life that matters. These desires are not random; God placed them in you for a purpose.

However, the key is that we are not meant to chase these dreams alone. We are called to pray over them continually, intentionally, and faithfully. Through prayer, our ambitions are reshaped by God's will and covered in His wisdom.

Psalm 20:4 says, "May he give you the desire of your heart and make all your plans succeed." This verse is not a blank check; instead, it reminds us that when our hearts align with His, our desires begin to reflect His goodness. Through prayer, He refines our wants into His will for our lives.

Proverbs 16:3 instructs us: "Commit to the Lord whatever you do, and he will establish your plans." This is more than a motivational quote; it serves as a blueprint for dreaming with God. Prayer is not about forcing our plans to succeed; it is about inviting God into the process and trusting Him with the outcome.

When we pray over our goals, we say, "God, this is what I hope for, but your will is more important." Our surrender is not a sign of weakness; it is wisdom. It protects us from chasing empty ambitions and helps us discern what is worth pursuing.

As a child, I dreamed of seeing my name in an encyclopedia (Yes, I was that kid!). Today, my dreams have changed: I want to raise my son to be a godly man, love my husband well, and serve God with my words. Though these goals may not be flashy, they are eternal, and I pray over them every day.

Praying for your dreams also provides the strength to keep going when doors close or timelines extend longer than expected. It serves as a reminder that you are not lagging. You are being prepared. And that preparation is part of the dream as well.

So, do not just set goals; saturate them in prayer. Allow God to shape your vision. Ask Him to close the wrong doors and open the right ones. Trust Him with the timing. Remember: a dream surrendered in prayer is never wasted. It transforms into something sacred, something far greater than we could ever plan on our own.

Praying Without Ceasing

"Rejoice always, pray without ceasing, give thanks in all circumstances; for this is the will of God in Christ Jesus for you." (1 Thessalonians 5:16–18).

Some people imagine prayer as something that only happens in silence, on bended knee, or during a designated quiet time.

But Scripture paints a much broader picture. Prayer is not just a discipline. It is a lifestyle. It is a continual connection with our Heavenly Father, a running conversation we carry with Him into every corner of our day.

To pray without ceasing does not mean we never stop talking to God, it means we never stop *inviting* Him in. Into our chaos, our celebrations, our routines, our car rides, our grocery trips. It is about making God our first thought, not our last resort.

Throughout my day, I whisper little prayers. "Help me respond with grace." "Be with my son as he takes his test." "Bless my husband's meeting today." "Thank You, God, for this moment." These are not long or fancy, but they are real. They are worship. They are surrender. They are constant.

Paul understood that life has hardships: persecution, pressure, doubt, and discouragement. That is why he did not just say *pray often*, he said *pray always*. In Ephesians 6:18, he echoes the same message: "And pray in the Spirit on all occasions with all kinds of prayers and requests… always keep on praying for all the Lord's people."

Prayer is our anchor, our rhythm, our spiritual breath. When we practice it consistently, through whispers, journaling, worship, and intercession, it becomes second nature. Prayer becomes as natural as breathing, as steady as walking, and as life-giving as love.

Romans 12:12 reminds us to be "joyful in hope, patient in affliction, faithful in prayer." Faithfulness is not driven by feelings, it is often about the simple act of showing up. We pray even when we do not feel like it, trusting that God meets us there. And as we learn to pray without ceasing, we bring our whole selves—our real, messy, beautiful lives—before Him and say, "God, be in this with me."

Unceasing prayer deepens intimacy with God. It heightens our spiritual sensitivity and gives us perspective when the world spins sideways. It draws us back to truth when our thoughts drift toward fear, pride, or envy. It strengthens our relationships, our patience, our trust. Most importantly, it reminds us that God is always nearby.

So, do not wait for the "perfect" moment to pray. Just start. Right where you are. Whisper thanks to your Heavenly Father. Ask for help. Praise Him in the hallway or the heartbreak. Keep the conversation going. That is what it means to pray along the way. Because at every moment, He is already listening.

Life Shaped by Prayer

Prayer is more than a moment; it is a method for a peaceful existence. It is how we stay tethered to God in the tension and the triumph. From whispered morning pleas to nighttime reflections, from bold requests to silent gratitude, prayer walks with us. It grounds us when we are lost, strengthens us when we are weak, and reminds us that peace is not found in our circumstances, but in God's presence.

To pray along the way is to keep your heart open to heaven through every season, through relapse and recovery, uncertainty and clarity, joy, and sorrow. It is not about mastering a formula. It is about surrendering in a relationship.

Here is the beautiful truth: when we stay in constant conversation with God, He changes us. Not just so we feel better, but so we can serve better. Because a life marked by prayer naturally flows into a life marked by service.

As you move forward from here, stay rooted in prayer, but do not stop there. In the next chapter, we will discuss what it means to serve along the way: to love, give, and show up for others not out of obligation, but as an outpouring of the love God is pouring into you. Let us keep walking and praying the path God has set before us.

Serve Along the Way

6

Finding Purpose as You Walk in Obedience

"If I know who the Shepherd is and how to find Him, it is surely my duty to do what I can to point other sheep to Him."

—Elisabeth Elliot

July 1996

Standing on a roof in the middle of July, I felt a gentle nudge in my heart. I heard the whisper of the Holy Spirit: "Don't you enjoy this, serving My people?" And I did. My seventeen-year-old heart swelled with love. God has a way of reminding us of the places where we feel closest to Him—even when we are far from living like it.

That week, I joined a group of fellow teenagers—plus plenty of adult supervision—on a mission trip to Memphis, Tennessee. We painted the interior and exterior of a widow's small home, then climbed onto the roof to finish repairs. As I hammered black shingles into place, something surprising happened: I was not afraid. I had always hated heights, but that day I stood steady, sure, and strangely fearless.

One of the most memorable parts of the house was the old RC Cola machine by the front door. All day long, curious neighbors stopped by for a cold drink and to ask questions.

"Where are y'all from?"

"Are y'all charging money?"

We greeted them with joy and explained with pride:

"No, ma'am. We are with a ministry sent by God to repair homes during the summer. It is completely free. All you must do is to apply."

Now, I was not exactly living a godly life back then. I was a wild teenager. But that week, God planted a seed in me. Twenty-nine years later, I still remember the presence of the Holy Spirit on that roof, and in my heart. That summer awakened something in me: the joy of serving others.

There is a rush that comes from serving in the Spirit, an overwhelming peace and joy that cannot be manufactured. It shows up only when we serve with humility, free of ego or expectation. As a teenager, I grew bored with sermons and Sunday school lessons, but mission trips lit me up. That is where I felt God the most.

Serving others keeps me grounded, and when my thoughts spiral, serving silences the chaos. You do not need to drop everything and join a mission trip to follow Jesus. Just look around your neighborhood. The elderly are some of the most overlooked people in our culture. Find a retired neighbor and offer a hug, a handful of flowers, or a plate of warm cookies. That visit may be the highlight of their week. That is how you become the hands and feet of Christ, by showing up with kindness.

Earlier today, I sat with a young woman just beginning her recovery. We prayed together. I shared my story first, so she would feel safe to share hers. While we talked, I was reminded again of how important it is to stay humble. Someone once did this for me. Now I will pass it on. I pray daily to be of service, and often, God sends someone who needs encouragement. But even when I am stuck in self-pity, I have learned to seek out ways to serve. It does not have to be grand. Simple acts still carry holy weight.

Sometimes, serving means heading overseas. But most days, it looks like this: I clean my kitchen. I love to cook, but cleaning? Not so much. Still, when life feels heavy, washing dishes helps. As I scrub a sheet pan or rinse a pot, I forget about myself. I stop obsessing. And when the kitchen is clean, I feel like I have conquered something. My husband is always thrilled too, his love language is an act of service. When I serve, my focus shifts. My peace returns.

Jesus is actions over words.

Jesus is actions over words. His miracles speak volumes: turning water into wine, flipping tables in the synagogue, healing a bleeding woman, raising the dead, washing His disciples' feet, and restoring the ear of the soldier who came to arrest Him. Even on the cross, Jesus poured out mercy. And His resurrection sealed our hope forever. That is the kind of servant I want to be—bold in love, humble in heart, and always moving toward the hurting. Service is medicine for my soul. It keeps me humble. It keeps me grateful. And most of all, it keeps me seeking God.

That moment on the roof was the spark, but over the years, I learned that service was not just about one week in Memphis. It was about living a lifestyle of love. The deeper my relationship with God grew, the more I saw service not just as an event, but as a calling, one that St. Francis described so beautifully in a prayer that has become my own heart's cry.

The Call to Serve

Lord, make me an instrument of your peace:

where there is hatred, let me sow love;

where there is injury, pardon;

where there is doubt, faith;

where there is despair, hope;

where there is darkness, light;

where there is sadness, joy.

O Divine Master, grant that I may not so much seek

to be consoled as to console,

to be understood as to understand,

to be loved as to love.

For it is in giving that we receive,

it is in pardoning that we are pardoned,

and it is in dying that we are born to eternal life.[9]

---

9 This anonymous prayer, commonly called *The Prayer of St. Francis*, was first published in 1912 in the French spiritual magazine *La Clochette*. For a historical study, see Christian Renoux, *The Origin of the Peace Prayer of St. Francis* (Paris: Éditions franciscaines, 2001).

I first heard this prayer in the rooms of recovery. It hit something deep within me. The words were not just beautiful. They were true. Every year, I ask someone to read this aloud on my sobriety birthday. It reminds me of where I have been and where I am going.

About a decade ago, I had the opportunity to walk the streets of Assisi, Italy, where St. Francis once lived. Born in 1181, Francis renounced his wealth and privilege to follow Christ in a life of radical poverty. He founded the Franciscan Order and became known for his humility, compassion for the poor, and deep love for all of God's creation. His legacy continues to shape my faith to this day.[10]

Although he did not write the Prayer of St. Francis himself, its words capture his heart and the heart of Christ. This universal message of peace and love was first published anonymously, centuries after his death, but it reflects the spirit of his life so closely that it has carried his name ever since. For me, its message is timeless: to seek peace, to offer love, and to live with open hands, just as Christ calls us to do.[11]

This prayer is more than a benediction; it is a call to live like Jesus. It begins with the plea, "Lord, make me an instrument of your peace," echoing Matthew 5:9: "Blessed are the peacemakers, for they will be called children of God." Peacemaking is not passive. It is the hard, holy work of healing, forgiving, and standing in the gap.[12]

---

10 "Prayer of St. Francis," in *The Complete Francis of Assisi: His Life, the Complete Writings, and The Little Flowers*, ed. Jon M. Sweeney (Brewster, MA: Paraclete Press, 2011)

11 Christian Renoux, "The Origin of the Peace Prayer of St. Francis," *Franciscan Archive*, accessed September 12, 2025, https://www.franciscan-archive.org/franciscana/peace.html.

12 Jack Wintz, "A Look at the Peace Prayer of St. Francis," *St. Anthony Messenger*, May 4, 2018, https://www.franciscanmedia.org/st-anthony-messenger/a-look-at-the-peace-prayer-of-st-francis/.

Each line contrasts what the world expects with what Christ calls us to: sow love instead of hate, offer pardon instead of holding grudges, shine light where others bring shadows. This is upside-down living, and it is the only way to real joy.

The line that always gets me is: "It is in giving that we receive; it is in pardoning that we are pardoned." Luke 6:38 says, "Give, and it will be given to you." True service is not about applause. It is about the quiet, soul-deep satisfaction of loving others well. As Jesus said in Mark 10:45, "Even the Son of Man did not come to be served, but to serve." That is our example.

Another section of the prayer echoes Philippians 2:3–4: "Do nothing out of selfish ambition … value others above yourselves." When we stop seeking attention and start paying attention—to God, to others, to where we are needed—we begin to live a life of real purpose.

The Prayer of St. Francis is not just for religious plaques and Pinterest boards. It is a blueprint for discipleship. When we live it out, when we choose to love, forgive, and serve—we become a reflection of Christ to a world in desperate need of hope. Before we rush out to serve the world, we must remember that love begins closest to us. The hardest, holiest, and most consistent opportunities to serve are often found right under our own roof.

Serve at Home

"Husbands, love your wives, just as Christ loved the church and gave himself up for her… In this same way, husbands ought to love their wives as their own bodies. He who loves his wife loves himself." (Ephesians 5:25–28).

Before we pack a suitcase or sign up for the next mission trip, let us ask a different question: What if our greatest ministry begins right at home? If we take the words of Jesus seriously. And if we were bold enough to pray something like the Prayer of St. Francis, we must start our service with the people we eat dinner with, fold laundry besides, and argue about thermostat settings with. That is where discipleship begins. That is where humility and compassion are put to the real test.

Jesus does not call us to skip over our own families while serving the world. He calls us to reflect on His love right where we are, within the walls of our own homes. When we serve those closest to us with joy, patience, and humility, we become living, breathing evidence of the Gospel.

The Bible does not treat love as an emotion to chase; it presents love as a decision, a daily, often inconvenient, act of the will. Paul makes it plain in Ephesians 5:25: "Husbands, love your wives, just as Christ loved the church and gave himself up for her." That is not soft, sentimental love. That is sacrificial, servant-hearted love, the kind that shows up when it is tired, overlooked, or frustrated. That is the kind of love that transforms households.

True Christ-like service means choosing others over us, not just once, but repeatedly. It looks like washing dishes without being asked. It looks like putting down your phone to really listen. It looks like grace when you could hold a grudge, or encouragement when someone else is barely hanging on. These small moments are not insignificant. They are sacred. Jesus proved that in John 13, when He knelt to wash the feet of His disciples, saying, "I have set you an example that you should do as I have done for you."

This example hits home, literally. It means we serve even when the work is invisible. Even when nobody says thank you. Even when our own needs feel unmet. Colossians 3:23–24 reframes it for us: "Whatever you do, work at it with all your heart, as working for the Lord, not for human masters … It is the Lord Christ you are serving."

When we clean the kitchen, pack school lunches, or stay up with a sick child, we are not just doing chores—we are worshiping.

Let us be real: sometimes it is easier to serve strangers than our own families. Familiarity can breed frustration.

But it is in that tension that God refines our hearts. Serving at home teaches us endurance. It softens our edges. It draws us into deeper dependence on Jesus, who knows exactly what it is like to love people who do not always appreciate the effort.

When believers serve with joy at home, they model the Gospel without needing a pulpit. Children learn more from a parent who lives out Jesus's love than from a thousand lectures about kindness. Marriages grow stronger not through grand romantic gestures, but through daily, quiet sacrifices that echo Christ's love for the Church.

Start small. Ask, "How can I love like Jesus today, in this house, with these people?" That is where the Kingdom breaks in. That is where transformation begins. When love flows freely in our homes, it naturally spills out into our neighborhoods. The people who live on our street or cross our paths daily are not there by accident; they are opportunities for compassion waiting to be noticed.

Serve Your Neighbors

"Jesus replied: "Love the Lord your God with all your heart and with all your soul and with all your mind. This is the first and greatest commandment. And the second is like it: "Love your neighbor as yourself. All the Law and the Prophets hang on these two commandments." (Matthew 22:37–40).

We do not have to look far to find a mission field. It begins right outside our front doors. I live in the historic district of a small Southern town, where our neighborhood rhythms feel like something out of a bygone era. A few times a year, we gather for block parties to reconnect, share news, and enjoy each other's company. When storms blow through, we show up with rakes and chainsaws to check on our elderly neighbors. We swap cookies, host porch dinners, and greet each other like old friends. When my mischievous dog Hadley sneaks off to visit her best friend Kilo down the street (which is often), I do not panic. I get a flood of friendly texts letting me know where she has been spotted. It is a sweet, simple network of shared life and mutual care. And it is exactly what God intended.

Serving your neighbor does not require a title or a complicated plan. It begins with a casserole. A kind word. A willingness to linger in conversation instead of rushing by. These moments may feel ordinary, but when offered with love, they become holy.

In Matthew 22:39, Jesus commands, "Love your neighbor as yourself." This is not a lofty ideal or a feel-good suggestion. It is the second greatest commandment, straight from the mouth of our Savior. And it is practical. It shows up in laughter, kindness, shared burdens, and borrowed sugar. God is not asking us to change the entire world in one dramatic gesture. He is asking us to be faithful to the people right in front of us. When we serve our neighbors, we are not just being "nice," we are being obedient. We are living out the Gospel in street-level, real-life ways.

Galatians 5:13 says, "Through love, serve one another." It is that simple. You do not need a passport or a platform to make an impact. All you need is love, a love that does not keep score or seek recognition. Paul reminds us that our freedom in Christ is not a license to live self-centered lives. It is an invitation to serve with joy. Service motivated by love does not drain us. It fills us. It does not demand performance; it flows from the overflow of God's goodness in our lives. And God has uniquely equipped each of us for this work.

"Each of you should use whatever gift you have received to serve others, as faithful stewards of God's grace in its various forms" (1 Peter 4:10). Some of us serve food. Others with conversation. Some with their hands, tools, and time. But all of it—every casserole, every front porch conversation, every leaf raked, or prayer whispered—is part of God's Kingdom work. You do not need to compare your service to anyone else's. You simply offer what you have, and God multiplies it. No act of love is wasted in His economy. Jesus reminds us in Matthew 5:16, "Let your light shine before others, so that they may see your good works and give glory to your Father in heaven."

When we serve our neighbors, we shine. We become living lanterns, pointing others to the goodness of God. They may not remember every word we say, but they will remember how we made them feel—seen, valued, and loved. You may not live in a small Southern town like me, but even in a high-rise apartment in a bustling city or on a busy suburban cul-de-sac, you can serve your neighbor with something as simple as a hello and a genuine smile.

In these verses, whether it is the command to love in Matthew 22, the freedom to serve in Galatians 5, the call to steward our gifts in 1 Peter 4, or the invitation to shine in Matthew 5—the message is clear: Serving your neighbor is not just achievable. It is divine. It is sacred, powerful, and glorifying to God. When we embrace the daily, sometimes messy, often unnoticed opportunities to love and serve, we fulfill His purpose in the most beautiful, tangible way. Just as we are called to love our literal neighbors, we are also called to love and serve our spiritual ones. Within the church family, God has placed us in community on purpose, each with a unique role to play in building up the body of Christ.

Serve Your Church Family

"We have different gifts, according to the grace given to each of us. If your gift is prophesying, then prophesy in accordance with your faith; if it is serving, then serve; if it is teaching, then teach; if it is to encourage, then give encouragement; if it is giving, then give generously; if it is to lead, do it diligently; if it is to show mercy, do it cheerfully." (Romans 12:6–8).

Serving does not stop at our doorsteps. It expands outward, to our church families. Church is more than a place we go. It is a living, breathing body, and each of us are a vital part of it.

Before you can serve well within your church, take time to discover how God has uniquely equipped you. Spiritual gift assessments can be a helpful tool, and many churches offer them to help members find their fit. Gifts like teaching, exhortation, leadership, mercy, or administration—each one is sacred when surrendered to God.

Personally, I have discovered that teaching is one of my spiritual gifts. I use it monthly in our church's Children's Ministry, and just last week, I had the joy of teaching Palm Sunday. As our little ones waved their green palm leaves and shouted "Hosanna!" I could feel the joy of heaven in that room. They were not just hearing the Gospel; they were experiencing it. There is something deeply sacred about bringing the story of Jesus to life for the next generation. That kind of service? It sticks with you. It fills you up even as you pour yourself out.

Once you have identified your gifts, start small. Bring a dish to the potluck. Volunteer for a day or two at Vacation Bible School. Join a Bible study or small group and offer to facilitate discussion now and then. If you love music, try out for the choir. Or maybe you are a behind-the-scenes person—helping with setup, slides, or sound. Consider mentoring someone younger over coffee or lunch. Every act of service contributes to the health of the body. But hear me clearly, you do not have to say yes to everything.

> **Overcommitting steals our joy of service.**

Overcommitting steals our joy of service. It is okay to say "not right now" when your spirit is not at peace. Pray before you say yes. If God does not give you clarity or peace, trust that He will raise up the right person for that role. Do not fill a position out of guilt. It may rob someone else of their opportunity to step into their calling with passion.

Romans 12:4–6 gives us the perfect reminder: "Just as each of us has one body with many members, and these members do not all have the same function … so in Christ, we who are many forms one body, and each member belongs to all the others." You do not have to be the eye, the hand, and the foot all at once. You just need to be faithful on your part. God created this diversity on purpose. Your contribution matters. Even though it feels small, it is essential.

Do not forget there is a time for everything. Ecclesiastes 3:1 reminds us, "There is a time for everything, and a season for every activity under the heavens." Sometimes, your season of service might look quieter, supporting others with prayer, presence, and encouragement rather than leading upfront. That is still service. And sometimes, your most obedient act is to rest. Jesus often withdrew to quiet places to be with the Father (Luke 5:16), and if He needed time to reset, you do too. Knowing when to step back is just as holy as knowing when to step up.

Paul echoes this wisdom in Galatians 6:9: "Let us not grow weary in doing good, for at the proper time we will reap a harvest if we do not give up." Burnout is real, and the enemy loves to twist our good intentions into distractions. Stay grounded in God's voice, not people's expectations. When we serve from alignment rather than anxiety, our "yes" becomes powerful. The harvest comes, not because we hustle harder, but because we stay faithful.

Even if you are walking through a season of church hurt, know this: God can and will help you heal if you ask Him. You may be in the middle of searching for a new church home, uncertain of where you belong. Or maybe you have stepped back for a while, unsure if you are ready to re-engage. Wherever you are, trust that God is always at work. He will lead you to the right community in His timing if you continue to seek His guidance. His guidance is the key to finding the right church community. God designed us for Christian fellowship. Sometimes it feels natural and joyful, and other times it may feel awkward or even painful—but do not give up. He is faithful, and His desire is for His people to walk together, encouraging, loving, and caring for one another.

When it comes to serving, remember, it is not about being seen, but about glorifying Him. Whether you are stacking chairs before Sunday service or teaching a Bible class, what matters most is the heart behind your service. Serve where you feel His pleasure, offering from a place of love, not guilt, fear, or obligation. God delights in obedience, not overextension. When service flows out of surrender, it becomes an act of worship. So let your gifts serve the church. Keep your heart open. And let it all—every word, every act, every offering—point back to Him. Because our service does not end at the church doors, it extends into our neighborhoods, workplaces, and communities. God calls us to be His hands and feet right where we are, every single day.

Serve Your Community

"Each of you should use whatever gift you have received to serve others, as faithful stewards of God's grace in its various forms." (1 Peter 4:10).

Serving does not stop at the church doors. It spills out into the streets, classrooms, neighborhoods, and courthouses. It touches strangers, systems, and schools. It transforms communities, one act of love at a time. One way I serve my community is through a local women's service club. Every year at Christmastime, we help families in need by providing gifts, groceries, and a dose of hope during what can be an overwhelming season. We present an anti-bullying puppet show to local elementary schools, and we award scholarships to students heading to college. When someone loses their home to fire, we organize clothing drives, collect essentials, and provide gift cards to help them rebuild. It is not flashy. It is faithful.

This club was founded back in 1914 as a humble sewing circle. The women made baby clothes for struggling mothers in our town. From the very beginning, their mission was clear. One of the founding members wrote these words during the club's first meeting:

> The desire to do a kindly, helpful deed is but the movement of the Spirit in our hearts, and if cultivated by us, may indeed grow into something wonderful and Christ-like as the years go by.
>
> —A. McD., *Christ Child Circle* founding minutes[13]

That line has stuck with me. It is a reminder that the nudge to serve, the impulse to help, is not random. It is the Holy Spirit at work. When we lean into that movement, even imperfectly, God grows something beautiful out of it. Jesus said the greatest commandments are to love God and to love your neighbor (Matthew 22:37–39). Serving others is one of the clearest ways to live out the second commandment. You do not have to make headlines to be effective. God does not ask us to fix the world. He simply asks us to be faithful right where He has planted us.

Community service can look like delivering groceries to a single mom, mowing an elderly neighbor's lawn, or offering a kind word to the cashier who seems worn down. It might mean tutoring a struggling student, showing up for a community clean-up, or just remembering someone's name and story. Romans 12:13 reminds us, "Share with the Lord's people who are in need. Practice hospitality." You do not need wealth or a title to live this out. You just need a willing heart.

---

13 *Christ Child Circle Yearbook, 2025–2026* (Eufaula, AL: Christ Child Circle, 2025–2026), unpublished internal record.

And do not underestimate the small stuff. I have seen how much power there is in a warm casserole, a handwritten note, or a smile offered at the right moment. These tiny seeds of kindness often bear fruit we never get to see—but God sees it all. Galatians 5:13 tells us, Through love, serve one another. When we serve with love—genuine, Spirit-led love—we are planting hope, building bridges, and showing people what grace looks like with skin on.

We also must remember this: service should flow from calling, not compulsion. Guilt-driven service wears us out. Spirit-led service fills us up. Ecclesiastes 3:1 reminds us there is a time for everything and that includes rest. Do not let burnout convince you that you are failing. Sometimes the holiest thing you can do is step back and ask, "Lord, what now? Where do You want me?"

Serving your community is about more than just meeting needs. It is about glorifying God. Every time you serve with humility and intention, you reflect His heart to a world that desperately needs it. Whether you are feeding a crowd or quietly checking on one neighbor, you are doing Kingdom work, and Kingdom work never goes unnoticed. Not by the people you help, and certainly not by the God who sees.

And sometimes, the most powerful service is the quietest. We do not always need a committee, a title, or a clipboard. Often, the way we live—our consistency, our integrity, our unseen faithfulness—becomes the example that points others to Christ.

Serve by Example

"You, my brothers and sisters, were called to be free.
But do not use your freedom to indulge the flesh; rather,
serve one another humbly in love." Galatians 5:13.

Serving others does not always mean feeding hundreds or washing feet. Sometimes, service is quiet, personal, and tucked into the fabric of daily life. You do not always need a schedule, spotlight, or plan. Sometimes, you simply serve by example.

Not long ago, after a twelve-step meeting, a dear friend pulled me aside and said, "Thank you for teaching me how to pray." I was stunned. I had not realized I was doing anything special. But she had noticed how I prayed before meals when we went out, how I opened and closed Bible studies in prayer, and how I asked for specific requests during the week so I could lift them up in my quiet time.

I was not preaching; I was just living. But in doing so, I served her. Without a sermon, without a lesson plan, I pointed her toward Jesus simply by being consistent in my walk. That is the beautiful thing about service: it often happens when we are just being faithful in the ordinary.

Jesus modeled this kind of quiet, intentional service. Yes, He performed miracles and spoke to crowds, but He also washed feet, welcomed children, and comforted the brokenhearted. In John 13:15, after washing His disciples' feet, He told them, "I have set you an example that you should do as I have done for you." He was not only talking about the act, but He was also teaching the heart behind it: humility, love, and presence.

When I think about that verse, it reminds me that I may never perform a miracle or speak to thousands, but I *can* serve through prayer, through presence, and through simple, faithful acts. And when others see that, they do not see *me*; they see Him. This kind of example-based service also keeps us grounded in authenticity. In a noisy world full of performative religion, people are craving real faith, lived out, not just being talked about. Matthew 5:16 reminds us, "… let your light shine before others, that they may see your good deeds and glorify your Father in heaven." Our quiet faith might be the light someone else needs. Not because we are trying to impress them, but because we are genuinely reflecting Jesus.

I think of the women in the Bible who served by example—Mary, the mother of Jesus, who followed God in quiet trust. Ruth, who remained loyal and hardworking in the face of uncertainty. In Titus 2:7, Paul instructs believers: "In everything set them an example by doing what is good." These women did not need a pulpit. Their lives spoke volumes. I want to live that way.

I want my children, my husband, my friends, my neighbors, and even strangers to see something steady and surrendered in me. Not for applause, but because it might help someone else walk a little closer to God. So, what do we do with all of this?

We start where we are. Because service is not just something we schedule. It is how we show up in the world. And when our thoughts get heavy or our purpose feels unclear, service brings us back to center. Back to Jesus. Back to the heart of it all.

The Power of Small Acts

Serving does not have to be big to be meaningful. In fact, small acts of kindness—done consistently and in love—are often the most powerful.

Here are just a few ways to serve others in your daily rhythm:

Simple, spontaneous acts:

- Send an encouraging text to your spouse, parents, kids, or friends

- Leave a sticky note that says "I love you" on the bathroom mirror

- Write a note of encouragement and slip it into your child's backpack

- Offer a sincere compliment

- Hold the door open

- Whisper a prayer for the person God places on your heart

Longer-term, intentional opportunities:

- Volunteer to read at a school or library

- Help serve meals at a shelter or soup kitchen

- Tutor a student after school

- Mentor a young woman at your church

- Visit someone in a nursing home or hospital

- Host a friend for coffee who needs to be heard

- Deliver a casserole to someone recovering from illness or grief

- Start a Bible study or teach Sunday School

- Be a greeter at your church on Sunday mornings

- Coach a little league team

- Drive a neighbor to a medical appointment

- Donate gently used clothes or school supplies to a foster care ministry

None of these things require perfection or performance. Just presence.

Service: The Way Back to Purpose

When negative thoughts start to creep in—when the enemy whispers lies about your worth or purpose, serve someone. If you are struggling with self-doubt, self-pity, or shame, shift the focus. Reach out. Encourage someone. Bring a meal. Buy school supplies for a foster child. Serve your way back into purpose.

Serving others does not just help *them*. It changes *you*. It pulls you out of your own head and into the heart of God. But do not serve to escape your pain or prove your worth. Serve because He first loved you. Serve because it is worship.

Just remember, you do not have to do everything all at once. Start small. Pray for God to show you one way to serve today. Then, maybe next month, take on something more. Let it grow naturally, from a place of joy and surrender.

Serving is not a side project of faith. It is the pathway of transformation. Whether you are offering a hug to a neighbor, teaching a Sunday school class, cleaning your kitchen, mentoring a friend, or simply praying aloud over a meal, you are reflecting the servant heart of Christ.

This chapter has shown that service is not one-size-fits-all:

- **Serve at home,** where love takes root and grows.

- **Serve your neighbors,** where small acts build bridges.

- **Serve your church family**, where the body of Christ functions best when each member plays their part.

- **Serve your community,** where the love of Jesus meets real-world needs.

- **Serve by example**, where quiet faithfulness leaves a lasting impact.

Let your life be the sermon. Let your love be the legacy. Let your service be your daily yes to a God who gave everything for you. Because when we serve others—we walk with Jesus.

But what happens when the road gets hard? When you are weary, anxious, or drifting from that daily yes? Staying connected to God is not always easy—especially when life feels loud or lonely. That is why in the next chapter, we will shift from the three pillars—surrender, prayer, and service—to five practical tools that help maintain a daily relationship with God. These are rhythms I rely on to keep me grounded in faith, even when I do not feel strong. From setting aside quiet time to taking meaningful action, these habits do not just keep me close to God—they keep me moving forward in faith.

Moving Forward in Faith

Navigating a Chaotic World While Staying Close to God

"Faith will get me anything, take me anywhere in the Kingdom of God—but without faith there can be no approach to God, no forgiveness, no deliverance, no communion… no spiritual life at all."

—A. W. Tozer, *The Pursuit of God*

October 2014

Officially divorced for a year, I finally felt ready to date again. I began to scan my familiar circles—Sunday mornings at church, midweek AA meetings, and the occasional scroll through social media—and noticed a few potential candidates. But being a Southern lady, I was not about to make the first move. Instead, I prayed. Every morning during my quiet time, I told God I was ready, but this time, I wanted Him to be in charge, not me. No forcing, no rushing, and no "helping" God along with my plan.

A few weeks later, a message popped up on Facebook from someone I had not heard from in years: West, a guy who used to live just down the street. He was originally from Eufaula but had moved away after his divorce two years earlier. I knew his parents from our church choir, so I was aware that he came from good people. After a day or two of casual chatting, I decided to give him my cell phone number.

What followed were two weeks filled with long, late-night conversations, the kind that leave you smiling even after you hang up. During those talks, I learned that West had just experienced a spiritual awakening. For the first time in his life, he was putting God first, and a newfound peace was taking root within him. When we finally decided to meet in person, West suggested mountain biking, which almost ended in disaster when I came close to tumbling down a steep trail. However, he was right there, steadying me and quite literally saving me from the fall. That adventure marked the beginning of the journey we are still on today.

In the years that followed, God blessed us with a beautiful, blended family, my fifteen-year-old stepdaughter, and my eight-year-old son—two incredible kids who fill our home with laughter, noise, and more joy than I ever imagined. Life under our roof is rarely quiet and often a little chaotic, but it is the good kind of chaos, the kind built on love, grace, and the daily decision to keep God at the center. Together, we have created a life that reflects His redemption, one where second chances turn into lasting blessings.

Over the past twelve years, I have progressed, anchored by three foundational pillars that sustain my relationship with God: surrender, prayer, and service. These are not just lofty spiritual ideals; they are the lifelines that have steadied me through every storm.

- **Surrender** helps me release control and trust God with the outcomes.

- **Prayer** keeps the lines of communication open between my heart and His.

- **Service** allows me to live out my faith with purpose, turning love into action.

These core practices—explored in Chapters 4, 5, and 6—have formed the spiritual structure of my life. They keep me grounded and remind me of what truly matters. But here is the truth: even with these pillars firmly in place, it is still easy to stumble. Why? Because most days are not marked by dramatic spiritual battles, they are filled with tiny, quiet tests of faith.

Interruptions. Irritations. That self-sabotaging inner dialogue. Those trivial things most often knock me off course. Hurtful comments and missed deadlines. A bad night's sleep. A heart that feels distracted or discouraged.

That is why I have learned I need more than spiritual pillars; I need daily tools. Practical, grace-filled habits that help me stay rooted when life pulls hard. These five essential tools are what I reach for when I need to realign, refocus, and return to God's presence:

- A **daily quiet time** helps me hear God's voice above the noise.

- The **"Start Your Day Over" rule** gives me grace to reset when the day goes sideways.

- **Key people** in my life keep me accountable, supported, and reminded that I am not alone.

- **Self-care** teaches me that rest is not indulgent—it is holy.

- **Taking meaningful action** gives me forward motion when I feel stuck or overwhelmed.

Together, these five tools support the spiritual structure already built on surrender, prayer, and service. Think of them as simple, tangible ways to tether your heart to God when the winds of life batter you. You do not have to master them all at once. Just start. Right where you are, with what you have.

God's not waiting for perfection. He is waiting for presence. These tools are not formulas for success; they are sacred rhythms for staying near to the One who never leaves your side. So, where do we begin? With one sacred practice: carving out daily quiet time with God.

Daily Quiet Time

One of the most powerful ways to stay connected to God and live out spiritual principles is by establishing a daily quiet time. This profound yet straightforward habit creates the space needed to hear God's voice, receive His peace, and align our hearts with His will. For me, quiet time has become more than just a routine—it is a lifeline. After entering treatment and rebuilding my relationship with God, I realized I could no longer afford to skip that daily connection. It has become the anchor that steadies me through recovery, motherhood, marriage, and ministry.

Since leaving rehab, I have started nearly every morning with intentional time in God's presence. This practice not only centers me; it transforms me. I begin with a devotional—whether from a book, an app, or an online source—then move into prayer. (I share my prayer outline in Chapter 5.) If time allows, I sit quietly and listen. In the stillness, I hear the gentle whispers of God most clearly. As 1 Kings 19:12 reminds us, God is not always in the wind, the earthquake, or the fire, but in the "gentle whisper." That whisper, which once seemed distant or impossible to hear, now brings comfort and clarity when the noise of life begins to rise.

Lost in addiction, the idea of dedicating my mornings to God never occurred to me. However, I now understand that peace comes from God. Without His guidance, I become reactive, overwhelmed, and scattered. That is why I encourage you to begin your quiet time routine. Start small—read a Psalm or a Proverb, use a devotional tailored to women's needs, or download a Bible app that offers daily readings. Set a reminder if necessary or find a devotional book and underline the passages that speak to your soul. The method matters less than the habit itself. And if you miss a day? Grace abounds. Just begin again. God's mercies are new every morning (Lamentations 3:22-23).

As your practice deepens, consider adding journaling. Use a notebook to record your prayers, thoughts, goals, and any impressions you believe come from God. When my mind is full of worry or fear, writing helps me surrender those feelings to Him. Journaling brings clarity to confusion and invites God into the messy places of the heart. I often use these questions to unpack my emotions:

- Am I afraid? What is the worst that could happen?

- Is my ego involved? What am I trying to prove? Who am I trying to impress?

- Am I resentful? Why?

After reflecting, I invite God in with prayer. If I am holding onto bitterness, I write out the names of those people and lift them to God, sometimes daily. There is one woman I have been praying for, on and off, for ten years, and I continue to do so, trusting that God is always at work, even when I cannot see the evidence.

I also bring my dreams and goals into my quiet time. When I feel stuck or unsure, I ask God to reveal whether a desire is from Him. I have learned to trust that He will open the right doors and close others. One sleepless night, I felt Him whisper to my heart: "I am removing people who are not truly your friends. It will feel uncomfortable. You will feel exposed and alone. But think of Michelangelo sculpting David—chipping away at the marble. That is your life with me. For you to become who I created, dust must fly, and pieces must fall." Such wisdom does not come through rushing or striving—it comes in stillness.

Quiet time is not about achieving a perfect spiritual moment every day. Some mornings are rushed, distracted, or dry—which is okay. God is not grading our performance; He is honoring our presence. Even when my thoughts are scattered, He meets me there. James 4:8 says, "Draw near to God, and He will draw near to you." That promise sustains me when the routine feels ordinary.

Over time, this simple daily act has changed everything. I no longer depend on fleeting spiritual highs. I am no longer waiting for inspiration to feel close to God. Instead, I am rooted, steady, and unshaken—and it all begins in the quiet. Still, even with an intense morning routine, some days can quickly unravel. That is why it is important to remember that with God, it is never too late to begin again—that is where the "Start Your Day Over" Rule comes in.

The "Start Your Day Over" Rule

Some days start with stillness, Scripture, and a steaming cup of coffee in hand. On other days, they begin with spilled milk, shouting matches, and a frantic search for lost keys. I have learned that even the most intentional mornings can veer off track—and when they do, I lean on my "Start Your Day Over" Rule.

This rule is not just a clever phrase; it is a sacred mindset rooted in the mercy of God. Each moment with Him offers a chance to begin again—not in our strength, but in His grace. God transcends the constraints of time, and we serve Him with awe and trust. His mercies are not only new each morning, but they are also new each moment we surrender ourselves back into His care.

Although I aim to start my days in quiet communion with the Lord, I must admit that I am no morning saint. I do not wake up humming hymns. But when I carve out that space to sit still with God, something sacred happens. My mind clears. My soul aligns. And on the days when life gets away from me, I do not spiral, I reset.

One particularly chaotic morning, my son resisted getting up; breakfast was a battle; the dog chased a squirrel; and I could not find my keys or my peace. I lost my temper. My son cried. Guilt crept in. The entire household felt heavy. But as we finally pulled out of the driveway, I paused and prayed aloud:

"God, please turn this day around. Help Grant have a good day at school. Let him be kind, and may others be kind to him as well. Help me to be patient and positive and use me to serve You today. We love you, Lord. Amen."

At that moment, something shifted. The chaos did not disappear, but my perspective shifted. My heart softened, and God's presence filled the space. The reset had begun. Starting over does not mean pretending nothing went wrong. It means acknowledging the mess, then placing it at God's feet.

These are the tools that help me do that:

1. **Prayer:** I speak honestly with God—He can manage my raw emotions.

2. **Scripture:** I anchor myself in truth, like 1 Peter 5:7: "Cast all your anxiety on Him because He cares for you."

3. **Movement:** A simple walk shifts my perspective—nature reminds me that beauty and order still exist.

4. **Community:** A trusted friend can reflect God's grace when I struggle to receive it myself.

Sometimes, I need all four. That is not weakness, it is wisdom. I am an emotional being. I love deeply, but I also wrestle deeply. Anger, insecurity, anxiety, they all show up uninvited. But when I choose peace over panic, grace over guilt, I am choosing to let Jesus lead me again.

Before my recovery, I often felt like the world was against me. If I had a rough morning, I wore that negativity throughout the day. I would fume, place blame, and isolate myself. Even in the initial stages of my sobriety, I found it difficult to reset my mindset. It took years for me to embrace God's grace and understand that a bad moment does not have to define my entire day.

- The "Start Your Day Over" rule can help you refocus every week, possibly even hourly. Using this myself, I have stopped expecting perfection. In the past, I would replay every mistake at night, obsessing over what I said, what I did not say, and what I should have done differently. The "mom guilt" often crept in, weighing me down with shame. Eventually, I realized I needed to extend myself the same grace that God gives me. Today, I use my flaws as motivation for growth. The only person expecting perfection from me was, in fact, myself. Since the beginning, God has used imperfect people to achieve extraordinary things. Noah got drunk. Sarah experienced jealousy. Moses was a murderer. David arranged a death to conceal his sin. Yet, despite their flaws, God called, used, and loved them. If He can use them, He can use me—and He can use you. His mercy allows us to begin again, regardless of the time, the mess, or the mistakes we have made. This rule is not about getting it right; it is about continually returning to Him, repeatedly.

- The "Start Your Day Over" Rule is not just a parenting tactic or a coping mechanism, it is a spiritual discipline rooted in the heart of the gospel. Jesus did not die so that we could strive for perfection. He died so we could live in grace. Every time we choose to start again—in the car, in a messy kitchen, in a muddy front yard—we proclaim this truth: God's love is greater than our worst mornings. His mercy is not limited to a once-a-day delivery. It flows endlessly, like the river in Psalm 46 that "makes glad the city of God." When I remember that, I breathe easier. I treat others better. I forgive myself quicker. And I keep going, not because I have mastered life, but because I have learned to reset it again, with the God who never gives up on me. Just as we need spiritual tools to reset our day, we also need key people in our lives who can remind us of God's grace and walk alongside us through the chaos.

Building Relationships with Key People

"And let us consider how we may spur one another on toward love and good deeds, not giving up meeting together, as some are in the habit of doing, but encouraging one another—and all the more as you see the Day approaching." (Hebrews 10:24-25).

> **Life is too short and too sacred to navigate alone.**

When the world feels overwhelming, the people God places in our lives help carry us through. Just as we need spiritual disciplines to ground us, we also need spiritual relationships to sustain us. Life is too short and too sacred to navigate alone. That is why it is essential to identify and intentionally nurture your "key people"—those God-given friendships that bring encouragement, accountability, and joy.

Do not let life get in the way. Set specific times to meet or talk on the phone; do not rely solely on texting as a means of communication. Ask meaningful questions, challenge each other, and speak honestly from the heart. Pray for one another and never assume you will have tomorrow to connect—reach out today.

Here are some of my key people: My friend Anna and I met at a Christian summer camp in fifth grade. Through divine intervention, our paths crossed again the following year, and we have now been friends for thirty-three years. Our connection is electric—God-ordained from the start. Often, I sense she needs prayer before we exchange a single word, and she will call me unexpectedly, saying, "God told me to call you." We were bridesmaids for one another, and when my son Grant was born prematurely, she dropped everything to be by my side. Her presence settles my spirit, and I thank God for her daily.

Then there is Kim. On the first day of high school, my Higher Power sent her straight to me. She had a firecracker personality and a heart full of compassion. We bent the rules, broke curfews, and built a sisterhood. She stood by me through rebellion, brokenness, and even addiction. When I finally confessed my alcoholism, she did not flinch—she cried with me. God knew I would need her steady love through it all.

Seventeen years ago, my friend Michele walked into my life, and I cannot imagine the journey without her. We first met when she married one of my co-workers, and what began as polite conversation at a work function quickly grew into a bond that has carried us through some of life's hardest seasons. When I went through my divorce, Michele became one of my fiercest cheerleaders. She and her husband wrote me letters while I was in rehab—letters soaked with grace, truth, and encouragement I clung to on the darkest days. Years later, when her husband suffered a massive heart attack, I stood beside her in hospital waiting rooms, praying, crying, and believing with her. Today, the tables have turned again, and I get to be the one clapping the loudest as she builds her business with courage and grit.

That is what key people do—they love without judgment, they show up without being asked, and they carry your burdens as if they were their own. Michele and I have a kind of friendship where we finish each other's sentences and read each other's moods without saying a word. She is my safe place, the person I can tell anything to and know I will receive encouragement and prayer—not criticism or shame. She is a steady rock in my life, and her presence is a daily reminder of God's kindness in giving us people who help us keep standing.

And then there's Lindsay, a God-given surprise. We worked together for years, and when my drinking spiraled, I pulled away. After treatment, I apologized, and she welcomed me with open arms. Our friendship deepened. When her son tragically passed away, I rushed to her side. Holding her hand in that grief, she whispered, "This is why you got sober." That moment sealed our bond into something eternal.

Since then, we have traveled to fun locations, shared tears, and laughter, and maintained a deep connection. Beyond these four women, I have a recovery circle that meets every Sunday. My sponsor, Amy, knows me deeply and loves me unconditionally. Katie H. brings joy and energy, while Amy C. brings wisdom and wit. These women are not competitors or critics but companions on the journey. I lift their names in prayer every morning, grateful for friendships that nourish rather than drain.

Of course, I have also experienced toxic relationships—people who encouraged gossip, comparison, and discontent. Thankfully, God helped me release those ties. They were painful but necessary lessons. Now, I am careful and prayerful about whom I allow into my inner circle. I look for alignment in values, spirit, and peace. I meet new women at church, in Bible studies, or through recovery groups, and I let God guide the connection. I do not force friendships anymore. I let them grow, or not, with grace. Just today, I had lunch with one of my key people, who filled me with fresh hope. I remembered that I am not alone in my daily doubts and insecurities. Key people do not just walk beside you—they lift you, listen to you, and remind you of who you are in Christ.

One meaningful way to discover your key people is by getting connected to a small group at your church. If you are longing for an authentic connection but are unsure where to start, this is a decisive first step. Committing to a small group offers benefits like these:

- **Child-led Community**–A place to be seen, heard, and known. You do not have to pretend or perform—just show up as you are.

- **Spiritual Growth**–Studying Scripture and discussing biblical truths with others deepens your understanding and strengthens your faith.

- **Accountability**–People who will lovingly challenge you to keep growing and stay rooted in God's Word, especially when life gets tough.

- **Shared Wisdom**–You gain insight from others' life experiences, mistakes, and victories. Someone else's testimony might be the encouragement you need.

- **Prayer Support**–You do not have to carry burdens alone. Your group will pray with you and for you, often in ways that bring comfort and clarity.

- **Safe Space for Vulnerability**–You can confess struggles, doubts, or setbacks in a grace-filled environment.

- **Encouragement and Hope**–Group members cheer you on when you are weary and celebrate with you when God moves.

- **Opportunities to Serve**–Small groups often organize service projects, helping you live out your faith in practical, community-focused ways.

- **Consistency and Routine**–Having a scheduled time to gather with believers keeps you spiritually grounded and connected.

- **Lasting Friendships**–Many lifelong friendships begin in small groups. These are the people who show up with casseroles, text you Scripture, and walk beside you through both triumph and tragedy.

Right after we joined a new church five years ago, we discovered that instead of traditional Sunday school, they encouraged home-based small groups—spaces for sharing meals, studying Scripture, and doing life together. Jill and Chris, new members like us, invited us in, and our "yes" became one of our greatest blessings. We gathered every Sunday night for four years—potluck dinners, open-hearted conversations, and children's laughter echoing in the next room. We did not just learn about the Bible. We lived it. When someone was hurting, we prayed.

When someone had news to celebrate, we celebrated. We became family. And even when life eventually pulled us in different directions, the friendships we made endured. Two of those friendships—Jill and Kasey—still walk closely with me. Kasey and I raise our kids together and pray for one another through the daily grind. Jill is a wise and faithful friend who always reminds me of the truth. These relationships did not happen overnight; they grew because we consistently showed up and let our guards down.

We are now part of a new Wednesday night group—different faces, but the same rhythm of grace. On Friday afternoons, I lead a women's Bible study where we delve into the Psalms and share honestly about our lives. This space has become a lifeline, reminding us that those women, in particular, need safe places to be known, encouraged, and supported in their faith.

Hebrews 10:24-25 encourages us: "Let us consider how we may spur one another on toward love and good deeds ... encouraging one another." Small groups fulfill this purpose. They remind us that we are valued, loved, and never alone.

Our son Grant is also learning what it means to belong—to show up for others while being surrounded by people who believe in him. This concept extends beyond adult friendships; it is about creating a lasting legacy. We are sowing seeds of faith and connection now that we pray will grow strong roots in his life for years to come.

One of my favorite signs in Alabama says, "Go to church, or the devil will get you!" It makes me laugh, but there is truth in it. The church roots us, while small groups remind us of our identity in Christ. Ecclesiastes 4:9-10 states, "Two are better than one ... if either falls, one can help the other up." You do not have to walk alone. Although the Holy Spirit is always present, sometimes we need human companionship.

If you feel lonely in your church or are struggling to find your place, do not give up. Your people are out there. Try again or take a bold step to start something new. It does not have to be perfectly just or prayerful. Whether it is around your kitchen table or a virtual Zoom call, God shows up when we gather in His name.

Last fall, I began leading a group of women writers through Called Creatives. What started as a Zoom group has evolved into a mastermind of women stepping out in faith. We laughed, cried, published books, launched podcasts, and formed bonds that feel sacred. At our in-person retreat this spring, the connection was undeniable; God was in our midst.

Community is not always easy, but it is always worth it. Do not let fear or a busy calendar take away what God wants to give you through others. Show up. Be brave. Be honest. And remember, in the company of believers, burdens feel lighter, joy runs deeper, and grace never runs out. Proper self-care does not end with personal routines—it flourishes when we open our hearts and lives to others.

Practicing Self Care

As women, we often give so much of ourselves to others—our families, our work, and our communities—that we neglect our own needs. However, the truth is that you cannot pour from an empty cup. Prioritizing your health, rest, and well-being is not selfish; it is essential. Even Jesus took time away from the crowds to rest and pray (Luke 5:16). If the Savior of the world was available for solitude and restoration, we should do the same.

As I have grown older, I have realized that I am not the mother, wife, or teacher I aspire to be when I am exhausted or overwhelmed. That is why I aim for eight hours of sleep each night—not just for rest, but to be fully present for those I love.

Daily movement is another cornerstone of my self-care routine. Here are some ideas to incorporate more into your life.

Simple Ways to Move Your Body Each Day

- Taking a 10-minute walk after meals—just around the block is enough to clear your mind.

- Turn on your favorite worship music and dance in the kitchen (yes, seriously!).

- Stretch your body first thing in the morning—reach high, touch your toes, roll your shoulders.

- Try a quick YouTube workout—no gym, no equipment, just your living room and a willing heart.

- Joining a local fitness or walking group—accountability makes movement more fun.

- Use the stairs instead of the elevator whenever possible.

- Set a timer to stand up and move every hour if you work at a desk.

- Walk and pray—turn your neighborhood stroll into quiet time with God.

- Do simple bodyweight exercises during TV commercials—squats, lunges, or wall push-ups.

- Play outside with your kids, pets, or grandkids—your joy counts as movement too!

I walk for at least thirty minutes each day—not to achieve a particular body image, but to clear my mind and connect with God. Sometimes I pray aloud; other times, I listen to uplifting words through faith-based podcasts. This practice strengthens not only my body but also my spirit.

Nutrition is another area I have begun to manage more intentionally. I focus on reducing processed foods and sugar while incorporating more fresh fruits and vegetables into our meals. Cooking at home has become both a health goal and a source of joy, allowing me to nourish my family and express a creative gift that God has given me. As 1 Corinthians 10:31 reminds us, "So whether you eat or drink or whatever you do, do it all for the glory of God."

Self-care encompasses more than just physical health; it includes building confidence and joy. I take vitamins, see a nutritionist, and maintain a skincare routine suited to my age and skin type. In the past, I wasted money on products that did not suit me or that I did not know how to use. Now, I collaborate with professionals who guide me and help me invest in things that genuinely are effective.

Good skincare not only brightens your face; it also uplifts your spirit. When I feel put-together and vibrant, I carry myself with more confidence and purpose. I also choose clothing that is flattering, age-appropriate, and comfortable. Practicality is key; I have learned to select items that fit my stage in life and my lifestyle, from wrinkle-resistant fabrics to comfortable shoes that I can wear all day.

I encourage you to invest in yourself with the same care and thoughtfulness that you give to others. Quality shoes, bags, and skincare products may seem like luxuries, but they can become tools for confidence and self-respect. You are worthy of care, just as much as anyone else in your household.

Having a child later in life has deepened my commitment to maintaining good health and being fully present. My son, Grant, is one of my biggest motivators to eat well, stay active, and keep my peace. At the same time, I have learned that taking a few hours of solitude or friendship makes me a better mother and wife.

Socializing is also a vital part of self-care. I make it a point to have dinner with friends twice a month, attend a women's Bible study every other week, and take an annual girls' trip. I am part of a monthly birthday club and regularly check in with my close friends. These moments of connection remind me that I am not alone and that joy and laughter are also forms of worship.

Self-help books and podcasts offer an additional layer of support and insight. Whether I am listening to a podcast about managing stress on my way to an appointment or reading a parenting book poolside after a challenging morning with my son, I am filling my mind with wisdom. That is self-care in action.

Some days, I need more than information—I need spiritual renewal. During my walks, I often listen to devotional podcasts that help me reconnect with God. His Word revives my heart and grounds my mind. As Proverbs 4:23 says, "Above all else, guard your heart, for everything you do flows from it." Self-care is one way I guard my heart, allowing me to live and love well.

Remember, caring for yourself is not a secondary task; it is a sacred responsibility. When you treat your body, mind, and spirit with the respect God intended, you thrive and glorify Him in the process. By embracing self-care as a spiritual discipline, you position yourself to serve others from a place of wholeness, not depletion.

My 25 Ways to Lavishly Love Yourself (Without Apology):

- Pedicure
- Manicure
- Bubble bath
- Massage
- Get your hair done
- Journaling or writing
- Facial
- Take a nap
- Go for a walk
- Go for a bike ride
- Date night with my husband
- Lunch or dinner with a key person
- Bible Study with key people
- Girls' night
- Girls' trip
- Get-a-way with my husband
- Read a book for fun
- Watch a fun movie or series
- Go to a movie
- Listen to a positive or self-help podcast
- Go to a concert or live music in your community.
- Go shopping

- Find a hobby like crocheting or cross-stitch

- Take art lessons

- Go antiquing

Self-care is not just about skincare or sleep; it is about nurturing your soul and building confidence in God. As women and caregivers, we often underestimate the depth of our love. When life gets hectic and mistakes happen, it is easy to forget that we are fully worthy of God's grace. The influence of social media often distorts our self-image through endless scrolling.

Many women are natural nurturers. During a Bible study, a friend pointed out that people often look to the mother figure when a child appears messy or the home is untidy. We carry invisible pressures—some we choose, while others are imposed by society. However, we are not meant to shoulder these burdens alone. God is always ready to help us bear the load.

> "For God so loved the world that he gave his one and
> only Son, that whoever believes in him shall not perish
> but have eternal life." (John 3:16).

You are loved. Let this truth shape the way you start each day. You do not have to earn God's love; it is freely given to you. In my teenage years and early adulthood, I sought worldly solutions to fill a spiritual void. I believed that relationships, travel, and even alcohol would bring me happiness, but they only left me feeling emptier. It was not until I surrendered everything to God during my journey to sobriety that I genuinely felt whole.

Like any meaningful relationship, our connection with God requires time and effort. The enemy may whisper lies: "You are not enough," "You have failed too often." Fight back with the truth. When you wake up in the morning, say aloud: "I am loved." This simple practice has changed my life.

"The Lord is compassionate and gracious, slow to anger, abounding in love. ... as far as the east is from the west, so far has he removed our transgressions from us" (Psalm 103:8, 12).

You are worthy—not because of what you do, but because of who God says you are. I once believed that attending church or doing good works would earn me God's favor and volunteered more to mask the guilt over my drinking. But I have learned that our worth is a gift, not a reward. Once I understood this, I could stop striving and start thriving.

"I praise you because I am fearfully and wonderfully made; your works are wonderful, I know that full well" (Psalm 139:14).

You are unique. God created you on purpose and for a purpose. He does not make mistakes. Let this truth settle in your heart. Stop comparing yourself to filtered images and idealized lives. You contribute something irreplaceable to your family, your community, and God's kingdom.

Self-care is about honoring the God who created your body, mind, and spirit. The most valid form of self-care begins with knowing who you are in Christ—chosen, cherished, and deeply loved. Step into your day knowing you are loved, worthy, and empowered. That is where true wholeness begins.

Reading about surrender, prayer, and service is not enough—God calls us to live them. It is essential not only to discuss change but also to take the next right step. If you have been carrying the weight of a problem that feels too big to fix or too painful to face, surrender, prayer, and action can become lifelines that truly shift things for you.

Taking Meaningful Action

"Dear children, let us not love with words or speech
but with actions and in truth." (1 John 3:18).

Eleven years ago, I found myself at rock bottom. My life was unraveling due to issues with alcohol and untreated high blood pressure, which were slowly destroying me and hurting those I loved most. In that moment, I prayed, surrendered, and, most importantly, acted. That moment of obedience changed everything for me, and it can change everything for you, too.

Action creates movement where stagnation once ruled. My spiritual health relies on a daily rhythm that steadies me: I start each morning with quiet prayer, attend twelve-step meetings regularly, serve—especially women in addiction recovery—and reach out to trusted friends for wisdom, accountability, and encouragement. My family and I attend church together, and I also volunteer in our faith community. These practices not only fill my time but also fill me with peace, strength, and perspective.

Eight years into my sobriety, I began focusing on my physical health. I was constantly tired, overweight, and ran down, so I surrendered once again. I got evaluated for food allergies, started walking daily, took vitamins, and changed how I nourished my body. I lost thirty pounds, but more importantly, I regained energy and clarity. The same pattern emerged: surrender, prayer, and steady action—one small choice at a time.

When I am tempted—whether it is about having a drink, skipping a workout, or indulging in food that I know will make me feel worse, I start with prayer. Then I act. I take a moment to ask myself, "What is the cost?" and remind myself of what I have gained: freedom, health, and peace. This clarity keeps me grounded.

I do not do this perfectly, and neither will you. Some days I miss walking. Sometimes I indulge in birthday cake (and I love birthday cake!). Occasionally, I forget my morning devotion. But I do not stay stuck. I pull out my phone, read a quick scripture, whisper a prayer of gratitude, and step back into my routine. That is grace in motion.

I remember a vacation in Mexico where I was surrounded by people I did not know well, sitting at a table filled with my biggest triggers: alcohol and dairy. I missed my son and felt isolated, wanting to cry—so I did. I stepped outside, called a friend, and let the tears flow. Her compassion wrapped around me like a warm blanket, and in that moment, the heaviness lifted. The enemy does not attack with firestorms but through small, quiet cracks. That is why action matters: reaching out, telling the truth, and inviting grace are how those cracks get sealed by God's love.

So, meet with God every day. Bring Him your worries, both big and small. Lay them down in surrender, cover them with prayer, and then take one step forward. When you do, life begins to feel lighter, and you will sense God's presence more clearly. If peace does not come right away, reach out to someone you trust. Let your community carry what you cannot.

> **No mountaintops needed, just the presence of today.**

No mountaintops needed, just the presence of today. Surrender, pray, serve, and then repeat. One faithful step at a time is how healing happens, how chains break, and how you stay found.

As I have grown spiritually, one truth has become increasingly clear: everyone is fighting some battle. Whether it is anxiety, shame, addiction, or simply the heaviness of daily life, the struggle is real. That is why we need practical, spiritual strategies to reset, not just once, but as often as necessary.

I know God is real; I feel the presence of the Holy Spirit. But I also recognize how subtly and persistently the enemy attacks. When I stumble, the temptation to spiral downward is very real. This is where the "Start Your Day Over" rule becomes so important. It is a lifeline, a reminder that grace is never far away.

For nearly twenty years, alcohol dictated my choices. But now, by God's grace, He leads my life. His mercy is not limited to new mornings; it meets me in every moment. I have learned that even one rough hour does not have to ruin the entire day. When things fall apart, I pause. I pray. I read Scripture. I move my body. I reach out to someone safe. Little by little, the heaviness begins to lift.

That is the power of surrender. Through quiet time, starting the day over, or simply taking one faithful step forward, God meets us right where we are, not where we think we should be. And that is enough. It is never too late. You are never too far gone. Grace is always within reach.

Each of these tools—daily quiet time, the "Start Your Day Over" practice, surrounding yourself with godly people, committing to self-care, and taking intentional action—flows from one foundational truth: God is with us, moment by moment. He does not demand performance; He invites us into His presence. We do not need perfect mornings or flawless routines; we need to show up.

So, start your day in stillness. And if it unravels, it begins again. Let your faith move beyond words and into daily choices. That is where transformation begins. That is how healing grows. You are becoming who God created you to be—not through giant leaps, but by faithful steps. Today will be a fresh start.

Found

Allowing Yourself to be Fully Known and Loved by God

"We should always remember that love is the highest gift of God."

—John Wesley

July 2013

Rock bottom was not the end. It was the beginning. To be found, I first had to be lost. That night, at my lowest point, God met me in the pit and lifted me out of the darkness. It was a moment of divine rescue, and I will forever be grateful. I may never have surrendered to God's will without that deep valley. But in my repentance, a miracle occurred. I was finally ready for transformation.

The inpatient facility was full when I went in for my consultation. They said they would call in a day or two when a spot opened. Two days later, the phone rang. I packed my suitcase with trembling hands, but my heart remained peaceful. As I drove, I sensed the Holy Spirit riding with me. The fear that once paralyzed me had melted away. God was in control. The moment I stepped through those front doors, peace swept over me. My secret was no longer mine to bear. I was not alone. My Father took my burden into His hands, and I finally believed He could fix me.

Change does not come easily. It takes effort. It takes surrender. One of the first truths I had to accept in recovery was that alcoholics and addicts lie to others and themselves. At rehab, they repeatedly ask you the same questions in diverse ways, looking for inconsistencies. But when I arrived, I had already laid down my lies. I was ready for help.

Have you ever told a lie so often that you started to believe it? I told myself—and others—that I did not have a problem. And I thought about it. But when I finally admitted that I was an alcoholic and cried out for help, God was able to enter in. That is when everything started to shift. I gave Him control.

God was with me, speaking through me, steadying me in uncertain moments. I was ready when we woke up at 5:00 a.m. on the second day. I met my roommate, Nicole, and our conversation was easy. We shared who we were, what brought us here, and the stories behind our surrender. Together, we began peeling back the painful layers of our rock bottoms.

We discussed what might lie ahead over breakfast, biscuits, and creamy gravy. We did not know what to expect, but I was not afraid. Have you ever stepped into the unknown and felt a sense of complete peace? That was me. For the first time in years, I trusted God completely. The chaos that had ruled my life quieted, replaced by a gentle, reassuring calm.

> "Then you will know the truth, and the truth will set
> you free." (John 8:32).

The truth can set you free, but it can also break you first. In my first group session, I took a deep breath when it was my turn. "Hi, my name is Ashley, and I am an alcoholic." Just saying it aloud released a weight I had carried for years. I stepped out of the darkness and into the light of the Spirit.

Speaking the truth was both humbling and empowering. Alcohol had ruled my choices for far too long. I had made mistakes

I needed to face and repair. Now, with God guiding me, I was ready to do the work. His presence gave me strength. I opened my mind and heart to His voice. I listened. I was ready to heal.

Have you ever admitted a hard truth and felt its grip loosen? That is what happened to me. Speaking the truth stripped addiction of its power. The enemy lost his hold.

Later, they handed out a book about alcoholism. One description hit me like a freight train — it said that regular drinkers do not have to think about stopping; they just do. That was my reality. I could no longer pretend. It hurt, but it was liberating. The truth gave me a clear path forward.

Healing meant tearing down the walls I had built. On the third day, I met with a psychiatrist. I walked in with my usual mask, smiling and pretending to be happy. But he saw right through it. "You are so angry," he said. "I do not know if I can help you." His words stunned me.

My mask cracked. "How do I get rid of it?" I asked. He looked at me gently and replied, "Pray. Ask God to take your anger." So I did that every single day.

In group therapy, I worked through years of disappointment, resentment, and the wreckage I had caused. Then came a letter from my mother. She compared me to her mother, who had died from alcoholism. She admitted that she could no longer be around me. That letter pierced my heart. It forced me to face the truth and move beyond self-pity.

Have you ever been confronted with the damage you caused? That was my moment. Recovery led me to a twelve-step program. Posters of the steps hung in nearly every room at rehab. Counselors reminded us that true freedom came from working the steps with a sponsor. That is where my real healing began.

"Create in me a clean heart, O God, and renew a right spirit within me" (Psalm 51:10).

God moves when we let Him.

God moves when we let Him. Leaving rehab was terrifying. For 28 days, I felt safe and protected by routine and structure. Now, I was stepping back into the real world, with all its temptations. But I was determined. That night, I attended a twelve-step meeting, found a sponsor, and began working on the steps.

I stayed busy, surrounded myself with strong women in recovery, and clung to God. I got divorced, and my ex-husband's classroom was next to mine at work. It was not easy, but I held my head high. God was working in my life—hour by hour—and I could feel it.

Temptation came, as it always does. One night, my ex-husband came by to divide our possessions. The conversation got heated, but that night taught me three powerful lessons:

1. I was capable of self-control.

2. Pausing before reacting could change everything.

3. Seeking wise counsel was essential.

"A gentle answer turns away wrath, but a harsh word stirs up anger" (Proverbs 15:1).

Resentment is poison. Do not drink it. My ex's classroom was a daily reminder of our broken past. But through God's grace, I learned to forgive. Eventually, we talked, we forgave each other, and we even became friends.

There was a season when we considered reconciliation. But after prayer, we realized God had other plans. He remarried and moved away, and I genuinely wished him well. God can heal even the deepest wounds. Sometimes that healing means letting go.

Have you ever sensed God nudging you toward change? He will close the doors you thought should stay open. He will make you uncomfortable, so you do not ignore Him. Change is hard, but it is the soil where growth happens.

What is the key to lasting transformation? Surrender. I admitted I did not have the answers. I reached out for help. I listened. I obeyed. That is when the true transformation began. I was no longer lost.

Being found can be terrifying. But it can also be the best thing that ever happened to you. When I was in control, I wrecked my life. When I surrendered control to God, He led me to peace, freedom, and joy.

You have just read some of the most vulnerable chapters of my story—how God sought me and found me in the darkest hour of my life. Rock bottom was not the end; it was the beginning. True transformation began the moment I surrendered. I stopped pretending. I stopped lying to others and myself. And in that honest surrender, God met me. The truth broke me wide open, but it also set me free.

When I finally invited God into every part of my life—no more closed doors or hidden corners—His constant presence became my source of strength. He gave me the courage to tell the truth about my past and to use it for something greater than shame. That truth shattered the grip addiction had on me. It cleared a path for healing. Slowly, the walls I had built to hide my alcoholism and carry my shame began to fall. I had to face the damage I had caused, but God did not leave me to face it alone. He walked me forward.

Here is what I have learned along the way, and maybe you need to hear this too:

- Temptation does not go away, but it does not have to win.

- God can heal even the wounds you have buried the deepest, but you must let Him in.

- Sometimes healing requires release: of people, of patterns, of what you thought life would be.

- Change is hard, but it is also holy, it is the soil where growth begins.

- Being found can feel terrifying at first, but it might just be the best thing that has ever happened to you.

Trust the Shepherd

Before July 24, 2013, my spiritual life was unstable. I believed in God and prayed, especially during tough times. Yet, I was still trying to manage the chaos on my own terms. I wanted peace without surrender, purpose without challenges, and I wanted Jesus in the passenger seat instead of behind the wheel.

That night, everything changed. I was done pretending. I knelt, not at a church altar, but in desperation. I asked God a question I had never dared to ask: What is wrong with me? The answer came like a whisper, yet it struck me like thunder: alcohol. That was it. One word, full of truth, and I could not unhear it. The silence that followed was not empty; it was sacred. It marked the beginning of everything.

That early morning, I surrendered completely. I did not negotiate or ask God to fix everyone else first. I simply said, "Take it, Lord. I cannot do this anymore." Then I got up and acted. That surrender unlocked a new beginning—one that brought me to the point of authoring this book, to share my truth and hopefully help someone else share theirs.

Jesus did not wait for me to clean myself up or find my way out of the pit. He came searching. He left the ninety-nine to find me, the one (Luke 15:4). I did not deserve it, nor did I even ask for it correctly. But mercy does not require proper etiquette; it meets us in the mess. That kind of love will break you open and rebuild you stronger.

I was hurt and tired, clinging to a life that was killing me. But when I finally let go, He met me with mercy, not condemnation. My surrender was not a display of weakness; it was a demonstration of strength.

Strength says, "I need help." It is doing the awkward thing, even when you are scared. Because of that moment, peace now fills my life, and purpose fuels my days. Hope colors everything.

If you are reading this and wondering if God still performs miracles, let me save you the suspense: He does. I know because I am one, and you can be one too. I pray that you have your awakening, that God's love stirs your heart in a way you cannot ignore. Do not brush off the stirring. Do not wait for rock bottom or convince yourself tomorrow will be better if you keep doing things the same way. When you feel a spark, do not let it fade. Fan it into a flame. Protect it, nurture it, and feed it with truth, community, Scripture, and prayer.

Take action. Surrender everything—your past, your pain, your pride, your plans. Lay it all down like an offering and invite Jesus into every detail. He can turn broken pieces into beauty. Just ask Him.

He can turn broken pieces into beauty.

> "Rejoice always, pray continually, give thanks in all circumstances; this is God's will for you in Christ Jesus." (1 Thessalonians 5:16–18)

Prayer is not just what got me sober; it is what keeps me anchored. It is my lifeline. When I start to drift, when old habits whisper, when doubts creep in, prayer pulls me back. You do not need fancy words or a perfect setting, just start talking to Him. He is already listening.

Gratitude will ground you. It can change the atmosphere of your heart faster than any self-help tip ever could. When life feels heavy, make a list of what is going right. Thank God for the breath in your lungs, the friend who texted back, the strength to show up one more day. Gratitude shifts your focus from what is missing to who is present.

This journey is not about perfection. You will mess up and fall short, but God is not after perfection; He is after your heart. This is a walk of daily surrender, honest prayer, and service to others. That is how we continue to find God and remain grounded in grace instead of stuck in guilt.

When you follow Him with an open heart, your path becomes clearer, and your steps grow steadier. Your light will shine brighter, not because you have everything together, but because you finally know Who is holding you together.

So, trust the process. Trust the Shepherd. He knows every detour and every valley. You are never lost to Him. His grace and love surround you, even on your worst day. Follow where He leads, and you will find peace. Not all at once, but step by step, breath by breath, day by day.

Being found was not just an event that occurred one night in July 2013; it is a choice I make every single day. I choose surrender over striving, presence over performance, and trust over control. Every time I stop trying to fix everything on my own and fall into His arms, healing finds me there. That is where hope resides.

And, my friend, this invitation is not just for me; it is for you as well. What would happen if you stopped running and hustling to keep everything together? What if you allowed yourself to be found? Because right there—in the quiet, in the surrender—you will discover the God who has never, not for one second, lost sight of you. And that, dear one, is where your true story begins.

Taking Inventory

As you have read these pages, you have begun to wonder about your own story.

Let me be clear: I did not author this book *just* for people who struggle with alcohol or drugs. I wrote it for anyone who has ever felt lost, stuck, ashamed, or spiritually empty. Maybe your struggle is not substance-related—it could be anxiety, people-pleasing, perfectionism, comparison, or the weight of an unresolved past. We all have something with which we are wrestling. But if, while reading my story, a quiet question has stirred inside you—*Could I have a problem?* —then, friend, this next section is for you.

I am not trying to be a counselor or turn this into a twelve-step meeting. But I would be doing you a disservice if I did not pause here and offer some space for honest reflection. For me, everything began to change when I stopped avoiding the truth and started asking the challenging questions.

If you think addiction might be part of your story, take a few minutes and consider the following questions:

- Do you find yourself turning to alcohol, pills, food, shopping, or other habits to numb pain or escape reality?

- Have you noticed this behavior affecting your relationships, your health, or your peace of mind?

- Is there a part of your life that feels out of control, something you have tried to stop but cannot seem to?

- Do you feel shame, secrecy, or guilt surrounding this part of your life?

- Has your habit grown over time, starting small, but now it feels like it owns you?

- Do you ever feel like you need more of it to feel okay?

- Have you made promises to yourself, or to others, that you did not keep?

- Did your struggle begin after a loss, betrayal, or season of deep pain?

- Have you ever thought, "Maybe this is a problem," but brushed it off?

- Are you afraid to imagine your life without it?

If you answered yes to several of these questions, please do not ignore that nudge. Reach out for help today. You are not alone, and you do not have to figure this out by yourself. Start by connecting with a recovery community near you:

Alcoholics Anonymous (AA) or **Narcotics Anonymous (NA)**: Visit aa.org or na.org to find a meeting in your area. Most local districts have websites with current schedules, meeting locations, and contact information.

You do not have to face this alone. Talk to someone you trust—a friend, pastor, counselor, or doctor. There is no shame in asking for help. There is great courage in choosing to heal.

Addiction rarely storms in; it sneaks in quietly. It promises comfort but leaves chaos in its wake. I know because it happened to me. But once I stopped running from the truth and faced it head-on, everything began to change.

If any part of this resonates with you, do not wait. Reach out. Find a local recovery support group, such as AA, NA, or Celebrate Recovery. These communities are everywhere, and they are truly lifesaving.

God has a plan for your life; do not miss it. Our Savior still performs miracles. I know this because I am living proof. If He can redeem my story, He can redeem yours as well.

Acknowledgments

This book exists because I did not walk this road alone.

To West, Cameron, Grant, Mom, Dad, and Lou—thank you for loving me through the mess, the doubts, and the breakthrough God brought in the end. You saw who I could become before I could see it myself.

To Lisa—thank you for speaking truth when I wanted to run, for asking the tough questions, and for reminding me that grace always gets the last word.

To Carre, Charlotte, Deborah, Erin, Lainey, Megan, Michelle, Morgan, Olesya, Rachael and Tara—thank you for reading my chapters, praying over me, calling, sending late-night texts, and showing up big with encouragement and holy stubbornness. Your presence was a lifeline.

To my dear friends Amy C., Amy M., Felisha, Jennifer, Katie, Lindsay, Michele, and Teresa—thank you for loving me through this journey and celebrating my victories like they were your own. God used each of you in a mighty way.

And to the reader—thank you for holding these pages in your hands. I pray something here reminds you that redemption is possible, even for you. Especially for you.

Author Resource Page

Connect with Ashley Martin at:

https://ashleymartinministry.com/

Or scan the code

Index

Works Cited

Andrade, Chittaranjan, and Rajiv Radhakrishnan. "Prayer and Healing: A Medical and Scientific Perspective on Randomized Controlled Trials." *Indian Journal of Psychiatry* 51, no. 4 (2009): 247–253. https://www.ncbi.nlm.nih.gov/pmc/articles/PMC2802370/.

Buss, David M., Mary Gomes, Dolly S. Higgins, and Karen Lauterbach. "Tactics of Manipulation." *Journal of Personality and Social Psychology* 52, no. 6 (June 1987): 1219-1229. https://doi.org/10.1037/0022-3514.52.6.1219

Christ Child Circle. *Yearbook, Christ Child Circle, 2025–2026*. Eufaula, AL: Christ Child Circle, 2025–2026.

Elliot, Elisabeth. *The Savage My Kinsman*. Ann Arbor, MI: Servant Publications, 1961.

Emmons, Robert A., and Michael E. McCullough. "Counting Blessings versus Burdens: An Experimental Investigation of Gratitude and Subjective Well-Being in Daily Life." *Journal of Personality and Social Psychology* 84, no. 2 (2003): 377–389.

Foster, Richard, and James Bryan Smith, eds. *Devotional Classics*. New York: HarperCollins, 1990.

Fox, Gregory R., et al. "Neural Correlates of Gratitude." *Frontiers in Psychology* 6 (2015): 1491. https://doi.org/10.3389/fpsyg.2015.01491.

Holy Bible, New International Version. Grand Rapids, MI: Zondervan, 2022. Originally published 1973, 1978, 1984, 2011 by Biblica, Inc.

Keller, Timothy. *Prayer: Experiencing Awe and Intimacy with God.* New York: Dutton, 2014.

Levin, Jeff. "How Faith Heals: A Theoretical Model." *Explore* 5, no. 2 (2009): 77–96. https://www.ncbi.nlm.nih.gov/pmc/articles/PMC2654362/.

Newberg, Andrew, and Mark Robert Waldman. *How God Changes Your Brain: Breakthrough Findings from a Leading Neuroscientist.* New York: Ballantine Books, 2009.

Niebuhr, Reinhold. *The Serenity Prayer. In The Essential Reinhold Niebuhr: Selected Essays and Addresses,* edited by Robert McAfee Brown, 251. New Haven, CT: Yale University Press, 1986.

"Prayer of St. Francis." *In The Complete Francis of Assisi: His Life, the Complete Writings, and The Little Flowers,* edited by Jon M. Sweeney, 399. Brewster, MA: Paraclete Press, 2011.

Renoux, Christian. "The Origin of the Peace Prayer of St. Francis." *Franciscan Archive.* Accessed September 12, 2025. https://www.franciscan-archive.org/franciscana/peace.html.

Schafler, Katherine Morgan. *The Perfectionist's Guide to Losing Control: A Path to Peace and Power.* New York, NY: Portfolio, 2023.

Voskamp, Ann. *The Broken Way.* Grand Rapids, MI: Zondervan, 2016.

Whittle, Lisa. *I Want God: How to Love Him with Your Whole Heart and Revive Your Soul.* Revised ed. Nashville: Thomas Nelson, 2024.

Wilson, Bill. *As Bill Sees It.* New York, NY: Alcoholics Anonymous World Services, 1967.

Zahn, Roland, et al. "The Neural Basis of Human Social Values: Evidence from Functional MRI." *Cerebral Cortex* 19, no. 2 (2009): 276–283. https://doi.org/10.1093/cercor/bhn080.

Wintz, Jack. "A Look at the Peace Prayer of St. Francis." *St. Anthony Messenger*, May 4, 2018. https://www.franciscanmedia.org/st-anthony-messenger/a-look-at-the-peace-prayer-of-st-francis/.

www.ingramcontent.com/pod-product-compliance
Lightning Source LLC
Chambersburg PA
CBHW021825090726
47818CB00077BA/54